the book of boro

TECHNIQUES AND PATTERNS INSPIRED BY
TRADITIONAL JAPANESE TEXTILES

SUSAN BRISCOE

DAVID & CHARLES

www.davidandcharles.com

contents

introduction

My interest in boro began in 1991 when I was an English teacher in northern Japan. The owner of the local antique shop gave me a bag of 'unsellable' old clothing, saying that it might do for patchwork. This included a work jacket about ninety years old, with a small boro repair on the front. I was touched by the care someone had taken to repair the fabric before making something new. I didn't cut it up! I began looking for other pieces, finding out more about boro and its many enthusiasts today.

The Japanese word *boro*, meaning 'rag', has become a popular term among international textile artists over the last twenty years or so. It is most often associated with clothing and household textiles that were pieced from recycled scraps and repeatedly patched as they were used, worn out and became ragged. The original boro items were made from necessity, by people in poor and remote regions where raw materials for new textiles were scarce and expensive. While some antique pieces include simple sashiko, boro is not a style of sashiko stitching. It is the embodiment of another currently popular Japanese term, *mottainai* ('don't waste!').

Nowadays, vintage boro is admired for its subtle colours and ragged textures, the abstract art effect of the patches and the enduring warmth of a unique handmade textile. Antique boro is becoming expensive and good examples are scarce, partly due to the interest of collectors but also because a lot of boro was simply used up, worn out or thrown away. It is a finite resource.

Inspired by these original boro pieces, many people want to make their own. The good news is that this is not difficult: it needs relatively few resources other than fabric scraps, needle and threads; no special skills are required; and there are almost no rules, other than an appreciation of original boro. With the passage of time, from everyday wear and tear, new creations will start to acquire a similar patina to old boro, too.

This book includes the basic techniques you need to create your own boro-inspired items, with a selection of projects large and small to get you started, inspired by my collection of antique boro but with a contemporary twist. To make boro patchwork base fabrics more quickly, I have used my sewing machine for piecing, but all visible stitches are made by hand, and, like the originals, these can be quite rough and imperfect at times. Boro techniques can also be used to repair existing items, such as jeans and other clothing.

Contemporary trends such as 'visible mending' and 'slow stitch' have embraced boro, although nowadays we are rarely stitching from necessity. Boro is ideal for showcasing treasured fabric scraps, reflecting ecological and sustainability issues. Its patina of time is harder to achieve instantly and is best gained through everyday use, but simple breakdown techniques can accelerate wear. Perhaps we can never simply 'make' boro on demand – it needs time and use to truly 'become' boro. Make it, use it, love it.

boro history

'Once something becomes the fabric of our memories, it moves from the material to the non-material in its importance. It becomes hard to part with.'

Sheila Cliffe, Japanese textile researcher and kimono stylist

the meaning of boro

The kanji characters for *boro* also read as *ranru*, meaning 'rag', 'scrap', 'tattered clothes', 'a defect', 'run-down' or 'shabby'. While it has connotations of worthlessness and junk, to its original makers *boromono* (literally 'rag thing'), as it is sometimes called, represented a desire to lovingly clothe their families and keep them warm in very harsh environments, such as the remote farming areas of northern Japan. It was an everyday repair. They couldn't afford or access new fabric, so they used recycled cloth to make what they needed. Piecing, stitching and mending were once widespread throughout Japan, but remained important for longer in areas where new fabrics were not manufactured so were scarce and expensive. Layers of patches, worn and torn, created a random, tactile beauty.

The inside of this ragged, unlined hanten noragi ('half wear' work jacket) with makisode (wrapped sleeves) has raw-edge, heavily darned patches in shades of indigo. Tohoku, c.1900.

the second-hand cloth trade

Cotton cannot be grown in northern Tohoku, on Japan's main island, where winter is cold and long and the hot summer too short. Grown commercially in Japan since the 1600s, first as a luxury fibre, it was cultivated south of the Aizu region by the early nineteenth century and traded second hand around Japan. Before mechanized spinning and weaving, second-hand fabric was valuable. The far north of Tohoku and the western coast were supplied by sea via the *Kitamaesen* (north front route), linking the Kansai region (around Kyoto) with the northwestern coast of Tohoku. Ships travelled the route once a year, leaving Osaka at the beginning of April, and traded all along the coast as far as Hokkaido.

Generally, *kimono* (which simply means 'wearing thing') are modular garments, made from a series of rectangles with no shaping, so recycling is easy. Even the V-shaped front opening, where the long collar is attached diagonally, is not cut, and the fabric is folded into the collar to give extra bulk and body. One kimono uses one whole bolt of narrow cloth (*tan*), approximately 13¾–15in (35–38cm) wide and 36–38ft (11–11.6m) long, sewn with a centre back seam. Simple shapes can be unpicked and the fabric pieces rearranged to even out wear, the back becoming the front or the sleeve's wrist opening being reattached to the body. Unpicked for washing and resewn, kimono fabric must have been frequently 'turned'. Removable, washable collar covers, often made from black sateen, were sewn on to protect the kimono collar from wear and to prevent stains from hair oil (used to fix the elaborate hairstyles of the Edo era [1605–1868]). The collar cover can still be seen today on all kimono, but now usually matches. One exception to the collar shaping seems to have been padded *noragi* (work wear), such as *donza* jackets, where the V-shape was cut, perhaps to eke out the fabric or reduce bulk from the wadding (batting).

In rural Aomori prefecture, while prosperous local landowners could buy a whole second-hand cotton kimono, poorer villagers could only afford *tsugi* (scraps). Five or six women would club together to buy a 48–52lb (22–24kg) bale of second-hand cloth from itinerant traders. They washed the dirty, damaged rags in lye, removing the worst of the grime by scrubbing with rough fish skins, and starched the scraps with rice water before grading them. The fabrics bore the marks of previous use, such as worn collar edges. While the worst of the scraps were torn into narrow strips to make *sakiori* (rag weave fabric), or plaited into rope, the better ones were pieced together as patchwork, or used to patch existing clothes and household textiles. As these 'new' creations became worn and patched in turn, the fabrics took on the imprint of the humans who used them and so became boro.

a boro collector

Japanese folklorist and archaeologist, Chuzaburo Tanaka (1933–2013), recorded a lot of information about boro and its makers. He collected boro and other historic items from his native Aomori prefecture over forty years, from the mid-twentieth century onwards, together with the memories of the now elderly creators. It is clear from his records that women treasured their scrap collections and valued the boro they made, despite wishing to forget the extreme levels of poverty and hardship they endured in the early twentieth century.

From 2009 to 2019, part of Tanaka's collection was displayed at the Amuse Museum, Tokyo, a 'live museum' that encouraged visitors to touch and experience the exhibits in unique, immersive displays. In addition to the permanent galleries, there were special exhibitions focusing on different parts of his collection, including boro. In the area in which he collected, the more remote parts of Aomori prefecture, new textiles were once very hard to acquire: the only fibre grown locally was hemp, which was time consuming and difficult to process, so second-hand fabrics were reused carefully. Some boro are thought to have been used by as many as four generations, and show the stitching of several different hands, some more skilled than others.

The body panels are all that remain of this handwoven striped cotton kimono, which has had boro patches quite crudely applied inside. Perhaps the sleeves and collar were removed to create another piece of boro. Tohoku, c.1900.

Strips torn from the most worn-out rags were woven into thick *sakiori* (rag weave fabric), used for obi (kimono belts), rugs and other items where the stiff fabric was an advantage. Tohoku, early twentieth century.

A boro *hanten noragi* work jacket includes many *tsugi* (fabric scraps), reassembled to create a new fabric from stripes and checks, before being patched again. The lining combines a valuable piece of *e-gasuri* (picture ikat) featuring a design of Buddhist scrolls on the left (as worn) with *zanshi ori* (leftover thread weaving) cotton. Tohoku, early twentieth century.

dyeing and weaving

Katazome (stencil dyeing), *tsutsugake* (freehand paste resist dyeing) and *shibori* (tie dyeing) were all popular dyeing techniques, while *shima* (striped), *koshi* (checked) and *kasuri* (ikat) patterns were woven with different arrangements of warp and weft colours. *Zanshi ori* (leftover thread weaving) used up the leftover threads that had been space dyed for different *kasuri* in a random checked effect. Scraps of all are found in old boro. By the early twentieth century, *meriyasu* (a fine wool jersey) and corduroy, a Western textile influence, were also used, and sometimes very utilitarian fabrics, such as pieces of hemp *kaya* mosquito netting. Hemp, known as *taima* or *asa* (a more general term for bast fibres), was cultivated, spun and woven even in the far north, but producing one bolt (36ft/11m) of cloth from scratch would have taken all winter. Fine hemp had been considered a luxury item since ancient times, used for festival clothes for the Emperor and summer clothing for the aristocracy, with coarser versions used by all. But second-hand cotton was warmer and softer to wear than hemp.

Indigo strengthens fibres and the residual smell of fermented indigo and ammonia used to dye it was believed to repel snakes and insects, including lice, fleas and mosquitoes. During the Edo era, sumptuary laws regulated what all classes of society could wear, and the peasant class was severely restricted in colour choice to fibres dyed with indigo. Japanese indigo (*Polygonum tinctorium*) can be grown even in northern areas to make an affordable dye. It strengthens the thread by coating it and dyes natural fibres easily. Consequently, boro textiles were predominantly indigo dyed, but brighter colours, like touches of red, are seen by the end of the nineteenth century, after sumptuary laws were repealed. Other boro colours include black, brown and darker shades, the everyday clothes of commoners.

boromono

All kinds of boro items were made. In terms of clothing, there were: *noragi* (work wear), which included kimono-like short jackets such as *hanten* and *donza*, *mompe* (women's baggy work pants), *tattsuke* (women's tight work leggings) and *momohiki* or *mataware* (men's pants with separate legs worn over a *fudonshi* or loincloth); *tanzen* (a padded kimono for home wear in winter); *tabi* (the Japanese 'socks', which resemble gloves for the feet); *tebukuro* (mittens) for winter wear outdoors; *maekake* (aprons), with and without bibs; *hadagi* (undershirts) and *koshimaki* (a short tied wrap-around skirt worn as women's underwear); while *omutsu* (diapers) were made for babies and the bedridden elderly. Tanaka has several *omutsu* that were prepared by his own grandmother for use in her extreme old age. While this may seem sad, it also typifies the determination of these rural people to prepare, plan and care.

Then there were the many items made for the home. *Futonji* were futon mattresses once stuffed with *shibi*, the soft part of rice straw, which was replaced annually. *Bodo* or *bodoko* were pieced boro cloths of different sizes, the name coming from the patchwork technique, *bodotsugi*. They could be used like bed sheets, placed straight on top of insulating straw, or made from numerous layers, like a thick patchwork quilt. Smaller *bodoko* were used as birthing cloths, to bless babies with good fortune from the spirits of their ancestors, passed down through the fabrics. Other bedding included *donja* and *yogi*, hugely oversized, heavily padded kimono, wadded with *okuso* (rough hemp waste) and weighing more than 26lb (12kg), which often had the whole family snuggled together beneath them for warmth in winter. *Shikimono* rugs and *kotatsugake*, a cover made for the *kotatsu* (a table with a charcoal heater underneath), also doubled up as bedding. *Komebukuro* (rice bags) and *asabukuro* (hemp bags) were made for storage. *Zokin* (cleaning rags) were the last stage in the recycling process; they were up to four layers thick and densely stitched, sometimes with *hitomezashi* (one-stitch sashiko) patterns. In short, just about anything you needed could be made from boro.

A thick *bodo* (boro cloth bedding sheet) resembling a quilt, made with fabric in various colours and patterns, including several stripes and *kasuri* ikats. The front is carefully co-ordinated stripes. Some fabrics appear more than once, which give an interesting balance to the asymmetric arrangement on the back. Tohoku, early twentieth century.

Passed down through several generations, this *donza* work coat has worn away to just one layer in places, despite having multiple layers of fabric and two different sets of dense stitching holding them together. The upper body lining is hemp. The fabrics date from the late Edo period. *Donza* have extra front overlap panels, like kimono. Tohoku, second half of nineteenth century.

Various *zanshi ori* (leftover thread weaving) cotton plaids were combined to make this *yogi*, a kimono-shaped quilt. It is lined with a simple patchwork of indigo cottons. Tohoku, c.1900.

making boro

Because women were busy with farm work and raising their families, stitching was done in spare moments and during the winter, when the weather restricted outdoor work. Although they were stitching from necessity, they must have given careful thought to the placement of fabrics, their patterns and colours, as surviving boro often hint at quite a joyful use of scraps. More attractive fabrics seem to be placed decoratively in prominent positions. Holes were often carefully patched from the back, with similar fabric, so that the repair isn't obvious – the opposite of today's 'visible mending' ideas. The side of boro most often appreciated today for its 'abstract art' qualities is actually the back, as we are attracted by the apparently random placement of fabric patches.

Looking closely at old boro, *tsugi* (patches) were frequently seamed together as a patchwork, reconstructing a similar width to the original *tan* bolt, before being made into various items, with holes and worn sections patched along the way. Stitching was simple – running stitch, hemmed and raw-edged patches (appliqué), and occasionally herringbone stitch. The more elaborate patterns seen in Japanese sashiko are almost universally absent from old boro, although the thick thread, in limited shades of white and cream now dirty with age, plus indigo and black, is similar. Some boro pieces were stitched with thread unravelled from other textiles, and some with coarse hemp twine. As boro items wore out, more and more patches were added, both to the back and to the front.

becoming boro

Over time, with years of daily use, wear and tear, occasional washing, and the never-ending patching and repairing, boro takes on character with incredible textures and faded colours. This has sometimes been described as *wabi sabi*, the tea ceremony aesthetic where *wabi* is a kind of rustic simplicity and *sabi* a patina of age from repeated use, but boro is not part of the formal tea ritual. Yet it *is* a kind of patina, the imprint of many lives, with a simplicity and the abstract use of fabrics, that makes boro so appealing today.

Many but not all objects that possess *wabi* or *sabi* can be said to also have *shibui*, meaning a simple, subtle and unobtrusive beauty. While boro has the charm of everyday things, with its rough textures and subdued colours, we should not forget that its appeal is not universal, that the word means rags and is associated with dirt; some older Japanese people have negative memories of ragged kimono worn in their youth.

stitching for protection

Poverty aside, reusing textiles has a long tradition in Japan, for spiritual reasons as well as economic ones. Funzou-e kesa (Buddhist priests' mantles) made from rags and discarded fabrics were a symbol of humility, a physical expression of the monk's vow of poverty, stitched with prayers as an act of devotion. One funzou-e kesa in the Shousouin, the imperial repository at Nara, belonged to Emperor Shoumu, who abdicated in 749AD to become a monk. It is made from scraps of plain weave silk, with parallel lines of running stitch in purple silk thread, resembling raw-edge appliqué.

The way garments were constructed could confer special protection to the wearer. The kimono's centre back seam, for example, prevented evil spirits from attacking your most vulnerable point, at the centre of the back between the shoulders (also the location of the family crest on montsuki, or formal crested kimono). As children's kimono did not have a centre back seam, charms called *semamori* were embroidered at the same point for the same reason. In some parts of Japan, kimono and *juban* (under kimono) were pieced from collected fabric scraps for luck. Children's patchwork kimono, *hyaku toku* (hundred virtues), used scraps from family, friends and neighbours, and these were given to Shinjoji Temple, Kanazawa (also on the *Kitamaesen* coastal shipping route), in thanks for a child's good health. Many stitches and stitch patterns were also thought to have spiritual properties. In an age before modern medicine, people needed all the protection they could get. The power in stitches gave them comfort.

The patches repairing this portion of a *kasuri* (ikat) futon cover have been carefully chosen to blend with the pattern from the front, so the repairs are not so obvious. The effect from the back is far less controlled. *Kurume kasuri* fabric, from Kurume, Kyushu, Japan's main southern island, was popular throughout the country. Tohoku, first half of twentieth century.

This small *bodoko* has several large plain indigo patches, two on one side and a single patch on the other, all showing different degrees of wear. The origin is unkown, as it was found in a bundle of recycled fabrics bought at a Japanese flea market.

A plaited rope bundle, made from narrow strips of old cloth, contains fabric dating back to the mid-nineteenth century. Decades of grime and discolouration have given the cloth an amazing patina. Tohoku, early twentieth century.

boro today

Through Soetsu Yanagi's *Mingei* (People's Art) movement of the early twentieth century, the concept of *shibui* became more widely appreciated in Japan and overseas, and handmade things became appreciated anew. With Japan's rapid postwar modernization, rural society began to change with the redevelopment of towns and cities and the depopulation of the countryside. People became more mobile, the standard of living improved and resources such as fabric were no longer in short supply, even in more remote areas. People were encouraged to discard worn-out boro in order to hide the evidence of recent deep poverty in these isolated communities, and Tanaka reports that many boro items were buried or burned – sometimes at the insistence of younger family members. The boro items' elderly makers were reported as feeling a sense of shame, but also a sense of loss at seeing the disposal of items they had made with care.

It is difficult to pinpoint one particular exhibition or publication that began the revival of interest in boro and led to its reappraisal in the last quarter century. Certainly, Tanaka's work and the Amuse Museum brought boro to people's attention. His collection continues to be exhibited worldwide, while a new home is sought for it in Japan (the original Tokyo museum site is being redeveloped): the latest exhibition at the Japan Society in New York in the spring of 2020 presented antique boro alongside boro-inspired work by Japanese fashion designers Rei Kawakubo, Issey Miyake and Yohji Yamamoto.

Tadashi Morita, owner of a famous antique shop on Kotto Dori, Tokyo's 'antique street', amassed another important boro collection, which was included in the exhibition 'Boro, Threads of Life' at Somerset House, London, in 2014. Jointly curated by tribal art dealer Gordon Reece and Philipe Boudin of the Mingei Gallery, Paris, it posed the question 'Can art transcend function?'. Suggesting that we can still value boro that are 'products of an 'innocent eye', not 'cultured works of human artifice', it showed how people can make beautiful objects without art training, with limited resources and 'a spirit of adventure and imagination'. Large antique boro pieces were mounted on canvas stretchers, like paintings, and displayed against white gallery walls. The exhibition drew parallels between boro's blocks of colour and landscape, while considering the influence of similar 'primitive art' on twentieth-century abstract painters and artists who used discarded materials. Perhaps our knowledge of modern art means that we appreciate boro's abstract qualities more readily. This exhibition brought boro to greater public attention outside of Japan.

Morita, along with other antique textile dealers, and an active network of flea markets, including the monthly Todaji temple market in Kyoto and Tokyo's Setagaya Boroichi (a rag market held annually in December and January), provides old fabrics as raw material for modern stitchers, as well as antique pieces for collectors. The bookazine *Kofu ni Mise Rareta Kurashi* (Life Attracted to Old Cloth), 'a collection of examples of learning, making and enjoying with masters of old cloth', features lavishly illustrated, inspirational articles about crafters who work with old fabrics, plus an extensive shopping directory, and it often includes boro collectors.

Old fabrics have become popular with Japanese quilters like Shizuko Kuroha, who blends old fabric with innovative versions of traditional western quilting patterns. The annual Tokyo International Great Quilt Festival has a section of traders selling old cloth and the *Wa* (the ancient name for Japan) competitive category is full of quilts made with old fabric. While most quilts are far removed from boro, there are many boro-inspired works exhibited too. In 2019 Satoko Okamura won the *Wa* category with a large boro piece made of overlapped random rags, called 'To Mother' (*Haha E*), in memory of her mother's resourcefulness in life. She captured the very ragged nature of heavily worn boro and the quilt surface was made of tattered cloth fragments, held in place with a grid of stitches.

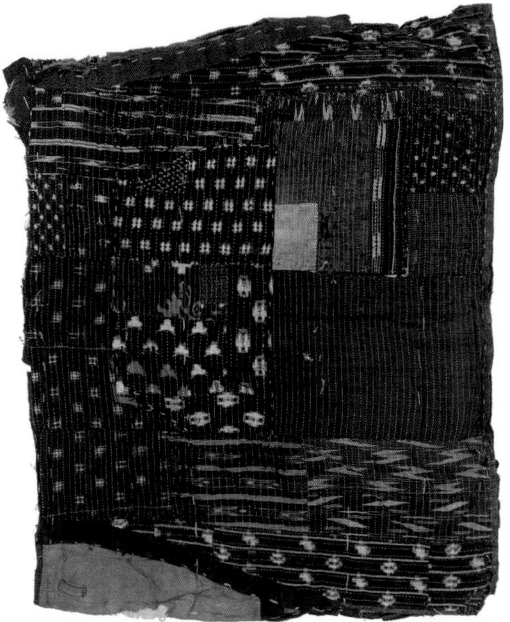

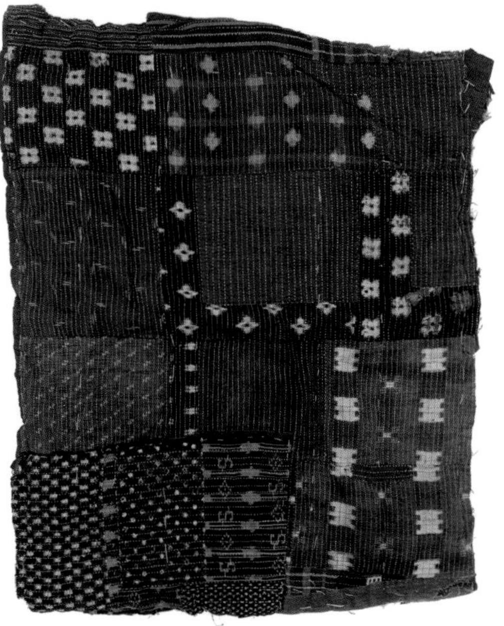

A very heavy *bodoko* sleeping mat for a child, made from two boro work jackets, with extra fabrics inside, including a pair of cotton Western-style trousers seen peeking out of the bottom left-hand corner in the top photo. Each jacket has dense vertical rows of very neat sashiko stitching, made much more skillfully than the *bodoko* itself. Tohoku, early twentieth century.

A boro cloth, possibly used as a *furoshiki* (wrapping cloth), made from firemen's old *happi* coats. The dyed circles and text give it a bold, abstract design. The right side of the fabric, pictured here, was used as the back; the seams are clearly visible. The wrong side of the fabric, used as the front, is more subdued. The text indicates it comes from Fukutsu village, north of Fukuoka, Kyushu. Early twentieth century.

Contemporary textile creators give boro a unique twist. Akiko Ike calls her version of boro, using very thick threads, 'chiku-chiku', an invented, onomatopoeic word for for the sound of the needle popping through fabric. Encouraging everyone to pick up a needle and stitch as they wish, Ike has taught and exhibited at textile shows in France and Australia. She is passionate about using recycled fabrics, including red and orange *juban* and kimono lining cottons that were once hidden, as well as *koinobori* (carp streamers) and celebratory flags. Another Japanese textile artist, Junko Maeda, has collected old fabrics for almost fifty years, using everything from *tenugi* (traditional narrow hand towels) to old *itajime shibori* (clamp resist dye) babies' diapers to create colourful works inspired by boro and Korean *bojagi* patchwork. She stitches with finer sashiko threads and frequently covers the fabric completely with simple *hitomezashi* patterns. Her work has been exhibited in the USA.

Layers of checked and plain patches on the back of this double-width panel from an old *futonji* (futon cover) suggest a strange, abstract landscape or map, with the patches resembling fields, roads and houses, with the striped blue cotton looking like the sea. Large-scale checks like these were popular patterns for household textiles. Tohoku, early twentieth century.

Contemporary fashion has embraced boro, merging it with the popularity of ripped and patched jeans. Japanese jeans brands, such as Kapital and Koromo, have used boro extensively, part of a growing international interest for concepts such as 'visible repair' and 'slow stitch'. Sustainability and mindfulness have become blended with making boro-inspired works as stitchers worldwide seek to create the unique. While the word 'boro' is sometimes used indiscriminately (often as a verb!), people do genuinely want to reference these old, ragged textiles in a positive way, using their own memories and treasured scraps. While strictly speaking these contemporary works are 'boro-inspired', it is often easier to just say 'boro' and #boro has become a social networking tag on the internet, with boro aficionados sharing photos and ideas through Facebook, Pinterest and Instagram. Boro has become international, yet still rooted in Japan, and stitchers often mix new reproductions of traditional Japanese fabrics with recycled cloth.

A big part of the appeal of boro is a passion for the tiniest fabric scraps, which can evoke memories, creating something new with them, and combining the meditative process of hand stitching with love. Tanaka recalled numerous visits to one elderly lady during his collecting years, just one of the many women who gave up their boro treasures. She said of her neatly wrapped bundle, 'These scraps have been like partners in my life. I have collected them ever since I got married: some were from my mother, but others were earned by my own efforts...' She recalled how her children would now reject boro as old and shameful. But of her precious fabrics, she said, 'I should have used them all instead of holding on to them'. Perhaps we should think of this when we create our boro-inspired work.

A modern patchwork throw inspired by antique boro, pieced from old indigo-dyed cotton fabrics. Antique indigo fabrics are in demand for all kinds of modern crafts with a vintage feeling. Bought at a craft market in Japan, c.2015, origin unknown.

Made by Japanese textile collector and *kasuri* (ikat) expert Izuho Horiuchi, this child's kimono is pieced from well-preserved handwoven cottons. Perhaps this is how *bodotsugi* (patchwork) boro garments originally looked, before becoming ragged boro? Late twentieth century.

tools and materials

Making boro needs very few tools, and the essentials, as well as the nice-to-haves, are outlined here. Your fabric and thread choices will influence the final look of boro-inspired pieces, from colour to pattern and texture. To make long-lasting items, as well as using scraps and worn fabrics, new or fairly unworn textiles will also be required, along with good strong threads, so let's explore your options.

essential tools

Some tools are absolute essentials, while others make your boro a little quicker or easier (see Useful Tools). If you are a quilter or dressmaker, you'll probably already have most of what you need.

Scissors: Keep a pair for cutting fabric only; smaller thread snips will also be useful.

Unpicker: Essential if you want to recycle fabric from old clothes.

Strong needles: Small and medium sashiko needles are ideal, as they don't bend and the longer eyes are easier to thread with medium and fine sashiko thread or similar thicker threads (see Threads). Use for tacking (basting) also.

Thimble: Thimble: For helping to get the needle through multiple layers of boro; choose one that is comfortable. There are two types of Japanese yubinuki thimble: a coin or palm thimble, made of metal or leather, which goes around the base of the middle finger on your sewing hand, and a ring thimble that is worn on the second joint of your middle finger (see Techniques: Stitching Boro for how to use Japanese thimbles).

Pins: Use fine, glass-headed pins to hold boro patches in place while you sew – these are less likely to be accidentally left in place beneath the patches.

Ruler: For measuring and marking fabric.

Marking chalk, pens or pencils: Choose an easy-to-remove marker that will show up on the fabric you are using.

Iron: Mainly to press seams with, although and iron is also useful for flattening persistent creases, such as unpicked seam allowances on recycled fabrics. Alternatively, use a pressing tool such as a seam roller or a wooden iron, which is sometimes used in quilting to press open seam allowances.

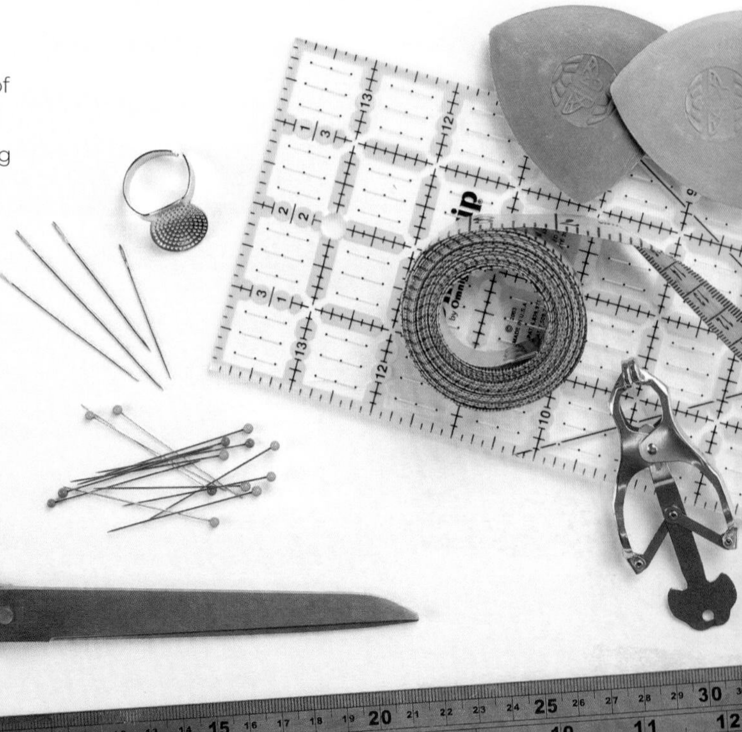

useful tools

Rotary cutter, quilter's ruler and cutting mat: Useful for cutting patches quickly, for trimming project pieces to specific sizes and for cutting pieces accurately and at 90-degree angles.

Sewing machine: You can sew all the projects completely by hand, but a machine makes project construction and patchwork piecing so much quicker; it doesn't need to be anything fancy, as only straight stitch and zigzag stitch are required.

Tape measure: Handy for measuring longer lengths on larger projects.

'Third hand': The *kakehari*, a traditional Japanese sewing tool, is a fabric clamp that tensions the fabric as you sew. Attach it to the fabric on the same side as your sewing hand (i.e. right for right-handers, left for left-handers) and fasten it to a table or chair with string or ribbon.

Storage basket: A container or bag to keep your sewing tools together is a good idea.

fabric

Originally borne out of necessity, nowadays boro-inspired projects can speak to our aims of sustainability for the planet. For many of the designs, I have used old (worn and recycled) fabrics together with new fabrics, using the newer materials for areas that might take a lot of wear and tear, or to act as a strong foundation for the older fabrics. Very weak fabrics will wear out quickly, so if you want your boro to last, combine these with stronger fabrics, and use them primarily to get the look of worn boro, on the visible side of your project. Natural fibres are easiest to work with and will become more beautiful with wear.

RECYCLED FABRICS

Recycled Japanese fabrics (including kimono) can be sourced online, or from Japanese flea markets or specialist sellers, but you can get a very similar appearance with many recycled fabrics found in charity shops or thrift stores. Woven checks and stripes look very similar to old Japanese fabrics. Low thread count, where you can see the weave, is easier to hand sew in multiple layers. Look out for cotton and cotton-blend woven clothing, as well as old linen tea towels, napkins and other worn but lightweight household textiles. Stretch fabrics, such as t-shirts, could be used for patches, but are not suitable for foundation fabrics and will be harder to sew. Most heavier furnishing fabrics are too thick for hand sewing, so are best avoided. Thick denim can be hard to sew in multiple layers, so use lightweight denim. Many Asian and other ethnic fabrics have the right kind of look, especially if they are indigo rather than bright colours. Don't forget, you can over-dye fabrics to get the shades you want (see Techniques: Dyeing Fabrics and Threads).

The quickest way to take apart old clothes is to simply cut them apart along the seam lines and discard the stitched seams and hems. But then the slight imprint of previous stitches, the wear and tear at the hem and the different rates of fading will all be lost – all things that will give immediate character to your boro. Take a little time to unpick the stitching – you will be rewarded with some very interesting edges and, if you are lucky, sections that almost seem to have shibori tie-dye effects from wear and fading. Patches from heavily worn areas of your recycled items can be darned onto your boro project, to instantly look like areas that have received a lot of wear.

Unpick shirts by removing the buttons, collar and button strip, then the sleeves. Remove waistbands from skirts and trousers, then unpick the rest: this can be time-consuming on the pockets and on areas of topstitch, but can yield interesting shapes and fades. Iron-on interfacing, in collars, cuffs, waistbands and button bands, can be left on or pulled off, leaving beads of glue behind, so be sure to use these scraps glue-side down. Handwash the unpicked pieces then press them, but not too flat – slight unevenness will start the boro 'wearing in' process a little quicker.

Second-hand kimono are even easier to unpick than Western clothing, as they are almost always handsewn with running stitch. Start by removing the collar and lining (if there is one) and then remove the sleeves. If the kimono is lined, the side and centre back seam allowances will be stitched togther from the inside, so remove this stitching too. Avoid more formal kimono, as these kinds of silk fabrics were never used for boro. Everyday kimono are less expensive to buy second hand than formal silk kimono, and have a more subdued style, appropriate for boro projects. Look out for silk *tsumugi* (raw silk) with a matte finish, wool *kasuri* (ikat) and other subtle fabrics. Really old Japanese fabrics, including *katazome* (stencil dyed), cotton *kasuri* (ikat) and natural indigo cloth, are sought after and relatively expensive, so use them sparingly. You can get a similar look with alternative materials or with reproduction fabrics.

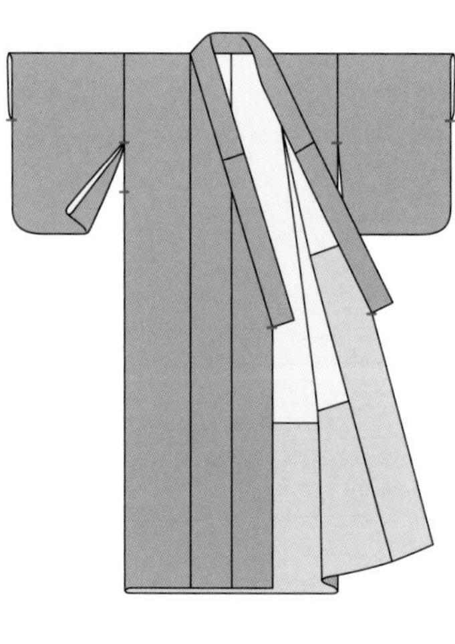

Fig 1a

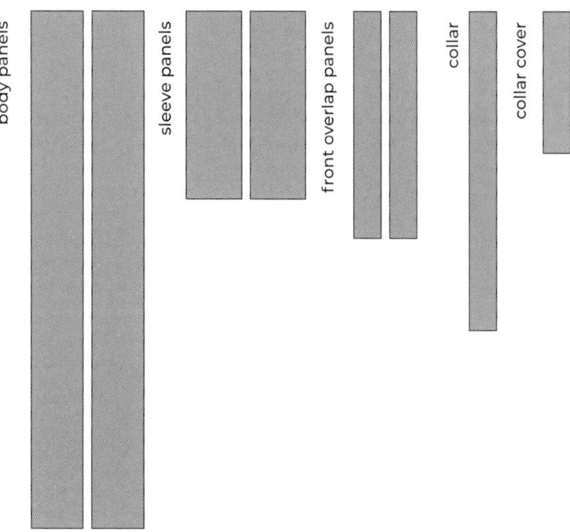

Fig 1b

An unpicked kimono yields a considerable amount of fabric. In Fig 1a, the red marks indicate where there will be tiny squares of reinforcing cloth inside the kimono seams, so be careful when unpicking these points. All the pieces will be rectangles (Fig 1b, not drawn to scale).

NEW FABRICS

There are many reproductions of antique Japanese fabrics available today. Stripes and checks tend to be woven, while *kasuri* (ikat) and shibori tie-dye patterns are usually printed to look like the originals, as these are expensive to produce. There are even faux patchwork and faux boro fabrics available. Pre-printed sashiko fabrics could be included, and the sashiko patterns stitched as part of the project. While patchwork fabrics are a good source of traditional Japanese patterns, for an authentic old boro look, steer clear of kimono-inspired, gold-print fabrics. Consider other ethnic textiles too, especially anything indigo dyed. Once your project is washed and used, new fabrics will quickly start to blend in with the old, getting a patina of age themselves.

FABRIC FIBRES

When choosing new fabric, be aware of how its composition can affect the look of your boro.

Cotton: Ideal for boro, can be washed and dyed easily.

Linen: Washes easily, but can fray a lot.

Cotton/linen blends: Ideal for boro, easy to stitch, wash and dye.

Hemp: Worn hemp is easier to stitch by hand than new hemp.

Raw silk: Low thread count so easy to sew, but frays easily.

Wool/wool blends: May shrink when washed – good for texture.

Cotton/poly blends: Only use if the thread count is low; high thread counts can be hard to stitch.

threads

When choosing thread for your boro stitching, it is important to consider its thickness, as bold lines add visual impact. Japanese sashiko thread, fine or medium, is excellent for this – look for larger skeins for best value as you will need a lot of it. Fine crochet cotton, no. 12 machine sewing thread and stronger embroidery threads, such as coton a broder, also work well. If you are using thicker threads, such as soft cotton embroidery thread or DK (sport) weight cotton yarn, a very large sashiko needle is best. While no. 12 or no. 8 perle embroidery thread looks slightly shiny, it can also work, but six-strand embroidery cotton (floss) won't be strong enough. If your chosen thread and needle combination is very difficult to get through the fabric layers, use a slightly larger needle or a finer thread. Try a few stitches to test your thread and fabric first, and be prepared to switch to a different thread if it is very hard to pull through.

You'll also need finer sewing threads for piecing and for sewing seams. It is always best to sew cotton with cotton thread, not polyester, which is so strong that it can cut through cotton fabrics.

techniques

Everything you need to know to make boro is covered in this section, including appliqué and patchwork techniques for creating boro-inspired textiles, with step-by-step guidance to stitching all the stitches used. Also covered are project construction techniques, as well as advice on ageing your projects for an authentic boro look.

making boro-inspired textiles

In essence, to create boro-inspired textiles, fabric patches are appliquéd onto a background fabric. These fabric patches can be left with raw edges, or they can have turned under edges, and where there is a hole, they can be applied by reverse appliqué. The background fabric can be one single piece of fabric, or it can be pieced together to form a patchwork of scraps or strips. One item of old boro can include several different techniques.

RAW-EDGE PATCH APPLIQUÉ

This is the simplest method for applying fabric patches and was originally done mostly on the back. Pin a patch to the backing fabric and stitch it down with running stitch (see Traditional Boro Stitches). The stitching can go across or around the patch; in lines back and forth; in diagonal lines; or in square spirals. Stitching over the raw edge helps to stop the fabrics from fraying excessively in use. Where there are multiple patches, stitching lines can cross from one patch to another. Take care when stitching down many patches not to accidentally trap a pin under an adjacent patch. I find it is easiest to stitch down patches a few at a time, so that I don't have too many pins in place at the same time, otherwise the work can get a bit prickly to handle!

Old boro pieces often have the raw-edge patches on the back, which tends to be the side that people love nowadays, and raw-edge patches are very popular in contemporary boro-inspired work. Recycled fabric can often be torn quite easily and the slightly frayed edge adds another level of texture.

TURNED-EDGE PATCH APPLIQUÉ

The fronts of most old boro pieces usually have the patch edges turned under quite neatly, but you should remember that turning the edge under will add a little bulk around each patch, which can build up considerably if there are many patches. Running stitch, hem stitch or an appliqué hem stitch can be used to hold the turned edges in place, or use blanket stitch for a more contemporary effect (see Traditional Boro Stitches and Modern Boro Stitches).

Raw-edge patches are often on the back or inside of old boro rather than the front.

Patches sewn to the front of antique boro frequently have the edges turned under neatly.

REVERSE APPLIQUÉ PATCHES

Holes in old boro were often dealt with by making a reverse appliqué patch, which might be closely matched in colour. To do this, back the hole with a much larger piece of fabric, leaving its edges raw. Working from the right side, turn under the edges of the hole all around – you can do this with the point of the needle – before stitching them down. Running stitches are usually quite tiny and close to the edge, but an appliqué hem stitch is even neater, and as little as ⅛in (3mm) can be turned under (see Traditional Boro Stitches).

PATCHWORK FOR BORO

Many old pieces of boro were made from pieced scraps, with more patches being added as they became worn. These were usually reassembled into the width of the original *tan* (fabric bolt), 13¾–15in (35–38cm), and larger pieces were made by sewing strips together. Some of the patches would have been the full width, but many more would have been half-width pieces, from collars and collar covers, so required joining. Unless you are using only old Japanese fabrics, a different nominal strip width may be more economical, such as the 10¾in (27.3cm) strip width used for the sofa throw, which was made from modern fabric samples, and the 16½in (41.9cm) strip width used for the hanten jacket, to make it slightly wider to fit the larger frame of a person today. Sketching out an idea for a larger piece of boro can help you visualize how many strips you will need and approximately how long they will need to be.

When piecing, machine or hand sew fabrics together using a ⅜in (1cm) seam allowance, which is wider than the conventional patchwork seam allowance; this is because many fabrics suitable for boro tend to fray more than patchwork cottons, as they have lower thread counts or are more loosely woven. Press the seam allowances to one side.

Many old pieces of boro have a line of running stitch to hold the seam allowances in place, like the decorative topstitching on pieced seams of the hanten jacket. However, this is not always necessary if there will be more stitching through several layers that will stop the seam allowances from twisting, as is the case on the sofa throw, which is stitched 'in the ditch' through both layers along the seam lines.

Running stitches can also be added along any faux patchwork 'seams' to make them look pieced.

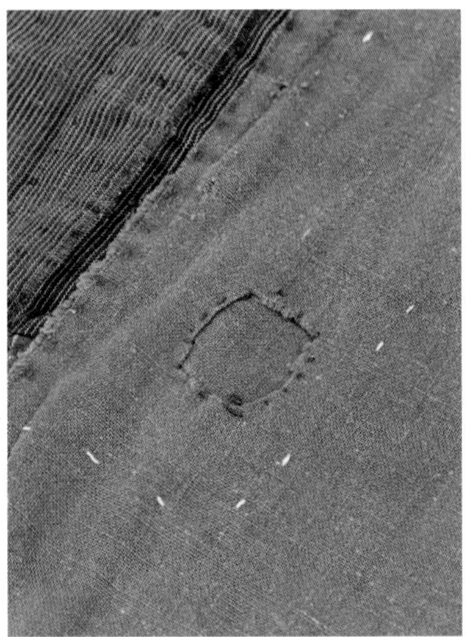

Reverse appliqué patches can be stitched with appliqué hem stitch or with tiny running stitches, as seen here.

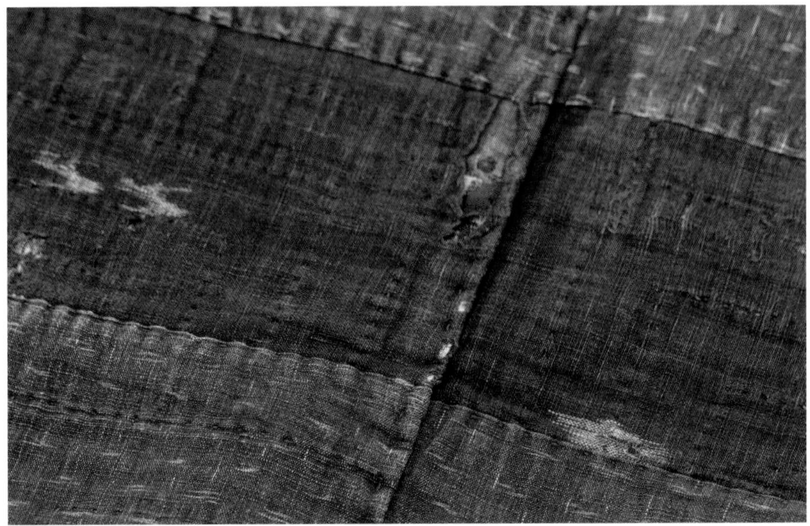

Patchwork seams are topstitched very close to the edge on this antique *donza* jacket.

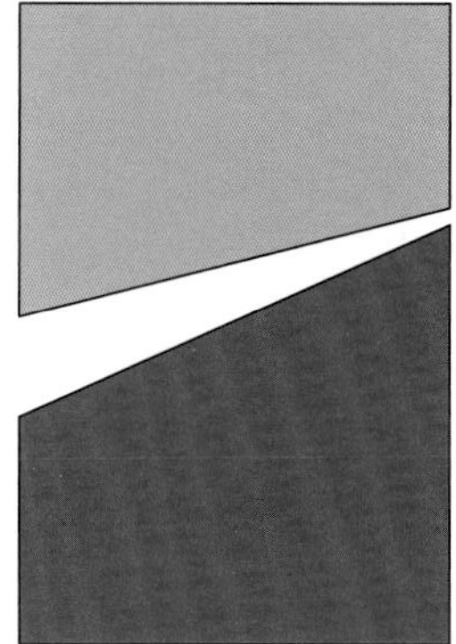
Fig 1a

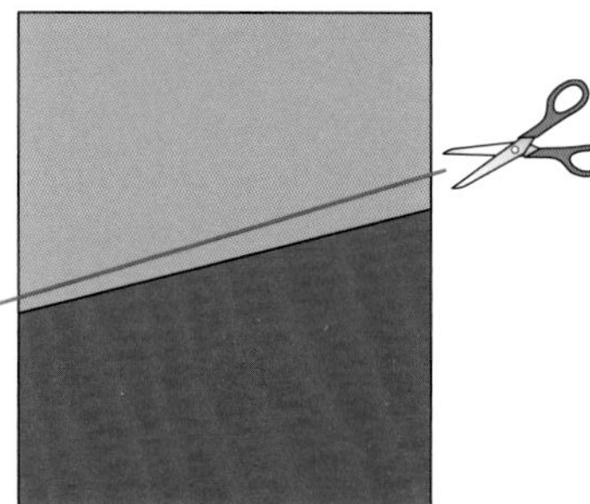
Fig 1b

Fig 1c

Fig 1d

Diagonal seams are rarely seen on old boro patchwork, as the shapes cut for making kimono are all rectangles. You may want to add a few diagonal seams for decorative effect, or to make use of recycled fabrics that have been cut on an angle. Take your two pieces of fabric (Fig 1a), place one on top of the other and make a diagonal cut across both, as shown by the red line in Fig 1b, to match up the angle on the edge of both pieces (Fig 1c). Pin the fabrics right sides together and sew, noting that they will need to line up at the ends of the stitching line, as shown in Fig 1d, not at the ends of the cut edge (which would put the finished edges out of alignment).

stitching boro

There are just a few stitches that are visible in old boro – running stitch, a simple hem/appliqué stitch (for reverse appliqué patches) and, very occasionally, herringbone stitch – while stitches such as backstitch, hem stitch and edge stitch hold the pieces together. Modern boro-inspired textiles, however, often include embroidery stitches for textural interest, including random cross stitch, blanket stitch and chain stitch, although you should be aware that any three-dimensional slightly raised stitch will not be so hard wearing. You'll find advice on working the stitches a little later (see Traditional Boro Stitches and Modern Boro Stitches), but let's look first at some more general stitching techniques. Unless shown otherwise, most stitches are sewn away from the hand holding the needle, so from right to left for right-handers and from left to right for left-handers.

STARTING AND FINISHING WITH A KNOT

Most stitches can be started and finished with a simple knot on the back; the knot can be hidden beneath fabric patches, or within the lining of the project, as on the hanten jacket, or 'popped' through and buried between layers, as on the sofa throw. For buried knots, tie two knots about ½in (1.3cm) apart at the end of the thread. Slip the needle into the fabric about 1in (2.5cm) away from the start of the stitching line. Bring the needle up where you want to start stitching and give the thread a couple of sharp tugs to pull the knots into the fabric layers. As you start stitching, your first few stitches will pierce the thread tail and hold it firmly.

To finish, tie a knot on the back by wrapping the thread around the needle, right against the back of the fabric. Put your thumb over the wrapped needle, to stop the knot running further up the thread, and gently pull the knot closed. If you need to hide the knot between layers, 'pop' the knot again. As knots are often visible on old boro due to wear, you could leave some on view, if you like that effect.

STARTING AND FINISHING WITHOUT A KNOT

Where running stitch needs to be very flat, as on the reversible bookmark, you can start and finish without a knot. Start stitching about 1½in (3.8cm) from where you want your stitching line to begin and stitch back towards the starting point. Turn and stitch back over your original stitches, piercing them occasionally (Fig 2a). At the end of the stitching line, turn and stitch back through the stitches over 1½in (3.8cm) (Fig 2b).

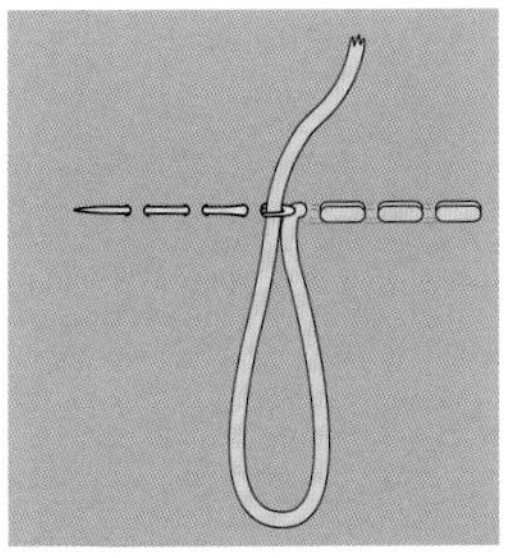

Fig 2a

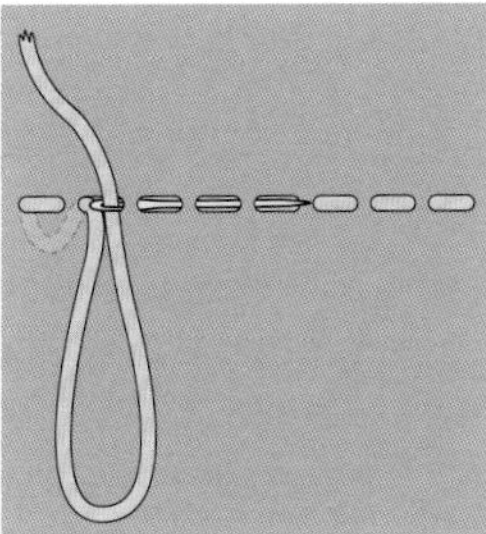

Fig 2b

USING TRADITIONAL JAPANESE THIMBLES

There are two kinds, both worn on your middle finger: a ring thimble, worn on the second joint of the finger and used with shorter needles (Fig 3a); and a coin or palm thimble, worn at the base of the finger and used with very long needles (Fig 3b). They require you to hold the needle quite differently from the way you are probably used to, and if you find this a strain, you can use an ordinary fingertip thimble instead. The coin thimble can be useful to push the needle through multiple layers or when stitching boro with denim.

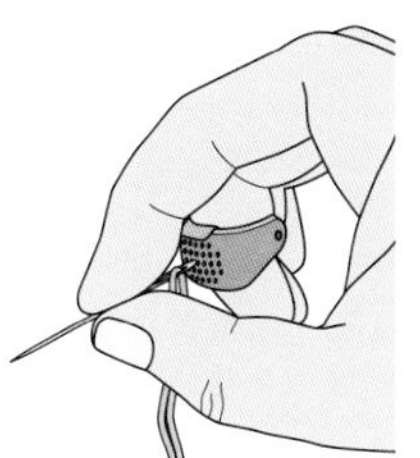

Fig 3a

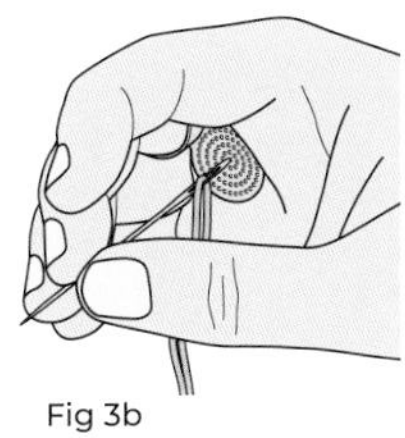

Fig 3b

USING A *KAKEHARI* CLIP

If you use Japanese thimbles to sew *unshin* running stitch the traditional way (see Traditional Boro Stitches), this is essential. The *kakehari* (cover needle) firmly holds the end of your fabric as you stitch (Fig 4). Clip it to the end of the fabric opposite to the direction in which you are sewing, and fasten it with a string or ribbon to a table or to a chair. It will enable you to stitch more quickly and to keep your stitching lines quite straight, even if you are not using a Japanese thimble.

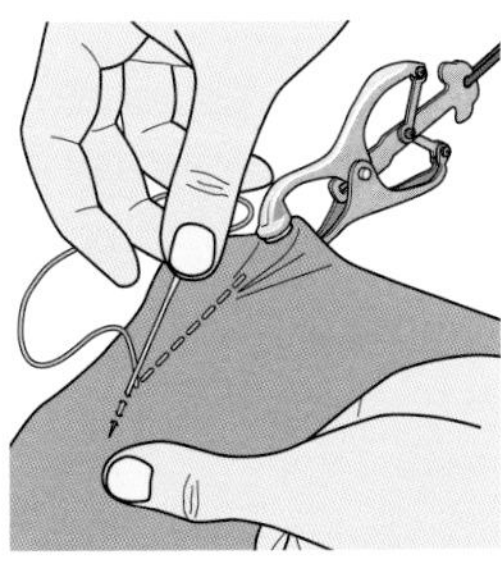

Fig 4

traditional boro stitches

RUNNING STITCH (*NAMI-NUI*)

This is the simplest stitch. It is used to sew patchwork pieces together by hand, for general construction, and to sew down boro patches (both raw-edge and turned-edge). Kimono are traditionally sewn with running-stitch seams, which can be removed easily to deconstruct the garment for washing. For boro, running stitches can be larger and more uneven, but for more functional uses, try to keep your running stitches around a scant ⅛in (2mm) long (Fig 5).

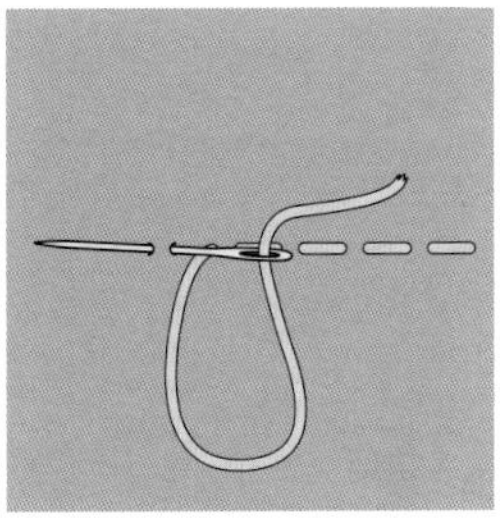

Fig 5

Traditionally, running stitch in Japan is sewn using a technique called *unshin*, which means 'moving needle', although it is the fabric that moves rather than the needle! The fabric is pleated onto the tip of the needle with an up-and-down motion (Fig 6); the needle is held quite still, usually with the eye end resting against a traditional thimble and the fabric held with a *kakehari* clip. Once several stitches are loaded onto the needle, the fabric is pulled off the back of the needle (rather than trying to push the needle through), with the fabric slightly gathered up by the thread. This is then eased out in a step called *itokoki,* or 'thread exhalation', which is rather like pulling out curtain gathers, by pushing the fabric along the thread. This stitching motion is essential if you are using a doubled thread for sashiko (see Simple Sashiko).

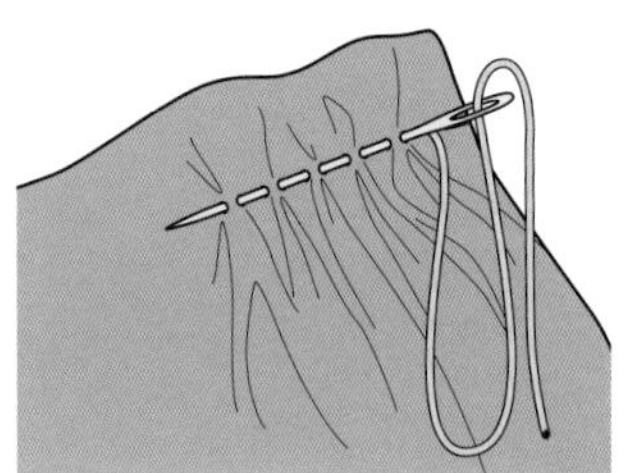

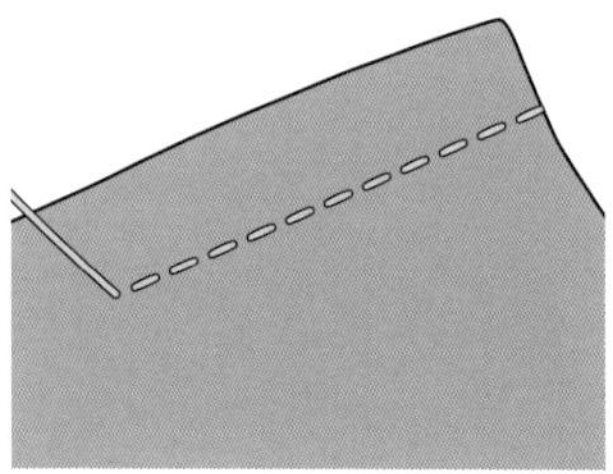

Fig 6

Stab stitches, used where too many fabric thicknesses make a traditional running stitch impossible, have a similar appearance. They are stitched individually in two steps – a down motion and an up motion – rather than in a single movement for each stitch. (Running stitches can also be sewn this way.)

Tacking (basting) is a temporary stitch that is really just a much longer running stitch, between ½in (1.3mm) and 1½in (3.8in) long. Use shorter stitches to hold layers together more firmly.

Multiple rows of running stitch were often used to create a stronger seam when stitching long lengths of narrow fabrics together. The idea was that if one set of stitches broke, the seam would still be held by the second set.

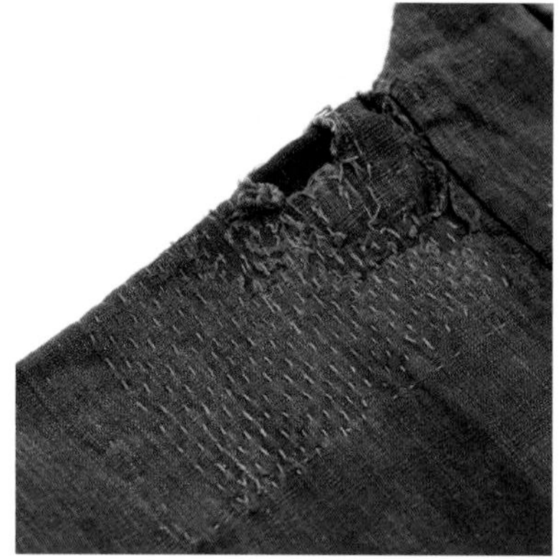

Row after row of running stitches sewn back and forth can be used to make a *kagaru* (darn) to strengthen fabric. Where the original fabric has worn very thin, an extra patch can be applied on the back – the start of a fabric becoming boro.

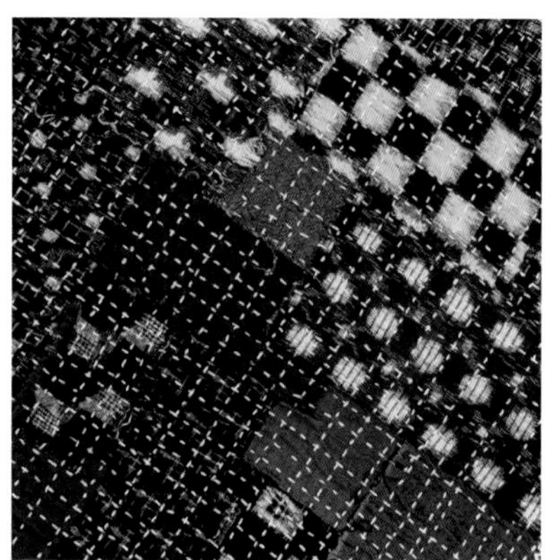

Running stitches can function as short tacking (basting) stitches but be left in place, as on the tote bag project. Start and finish sewing with a knot, tucked under the edge of a patch. Try to step your final running stitch over the top of the patch edge, to hold the raw edge in place and prevent excessive fraying.

BACKSTITCH (*HONGASESI-NUI*)

This is a stronger stitch than running stitch. The needle comes up through the fabric, then goes back down on the stitching line in the opposite direction – that is, backwards (Fig 7). Done correctly, backstitch seems to form a solid line and looks a little like straight machine sewing. It can be used in place of running stitch where a stronger seam is required, such as for the sides of the tote bag. Unlike running stitch, it will not unravel easily if cut through later. Half backstitch (*hangaesi-nui*), a slightly quicker seam option, is stitched in the same way, but the stitches on the top do not meet the previous stitch, so there is a small gap between stitches (Fig 8) and it uses less thread.

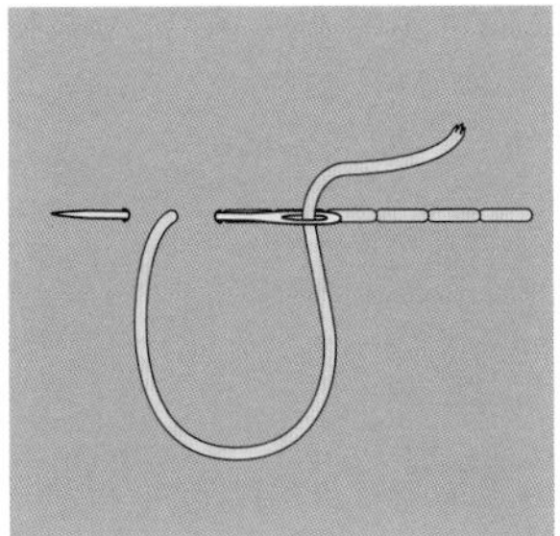

Fig 7

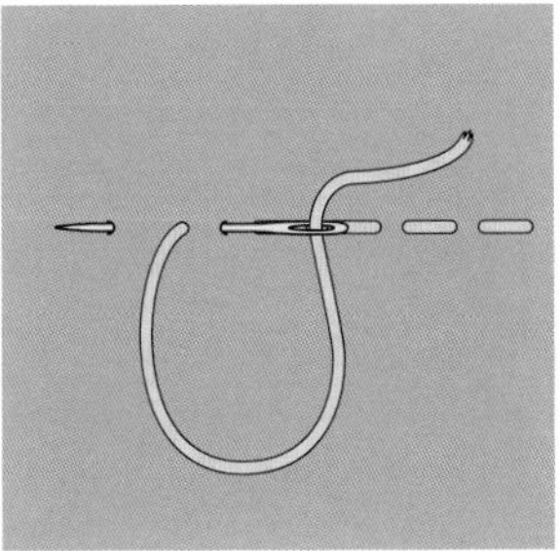

Fig 8

HERRINGBONE STITCH (*CHIDORI-GAKE*)

This is a useful stitch to sew down a raw edge that might fray more than you wish, or to join two pieces of boro stitching together. Unlike most of the other stitches included here, it is worked from left to right for right-handers and from right to left for left-handers.

Bring the needle up and take a stitch about ¼in (6mm) long, slanting to the right then push the needle in and take a horizontal stitch behind the fabric, in the opposite direction. Repeat. (See Fig 9.)

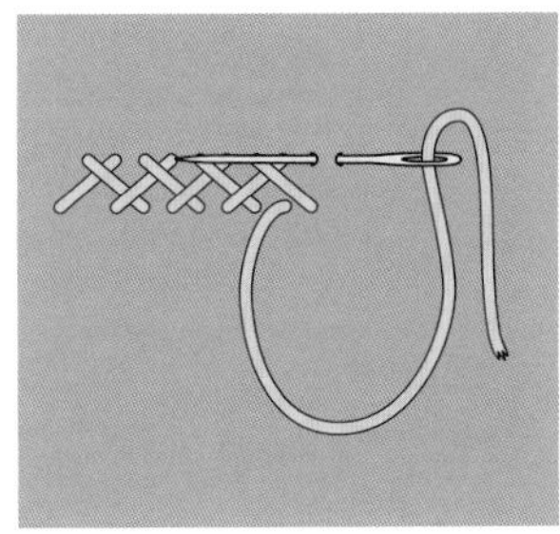

Fig 9

Herringbone stitch was used to add extra patches to the cuffs of the hanten jacket, where they are likely to get quite a lot of wear. The patch fabric is a tiny, precious scrap of antique *katazome* (stencil dyed) cotton.

APPLIQUÉ HEM STITCH

Appliqué hem stitch gives a very neat finish to patches. The needle comes up through the folded edge of the patch or hole, then straight down into the background fabric, before travelling along to the next stitch diagonally across the back, all in one move (Fig 10). Stitch away from the hand holding the needle.

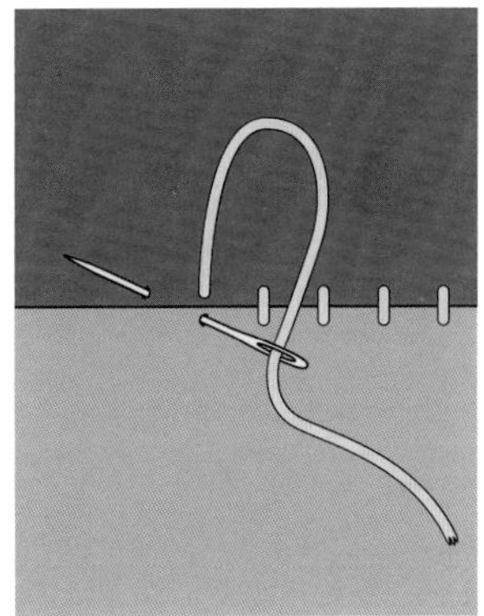

Fig 10

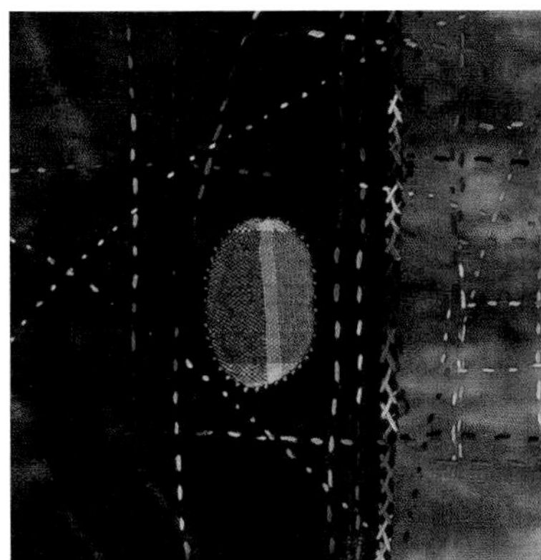

Appliqué hem stitch is a very neat way to finish a reverse appliqué patch, as seen on this detail from the table runner. The hole can be an irregular shape.

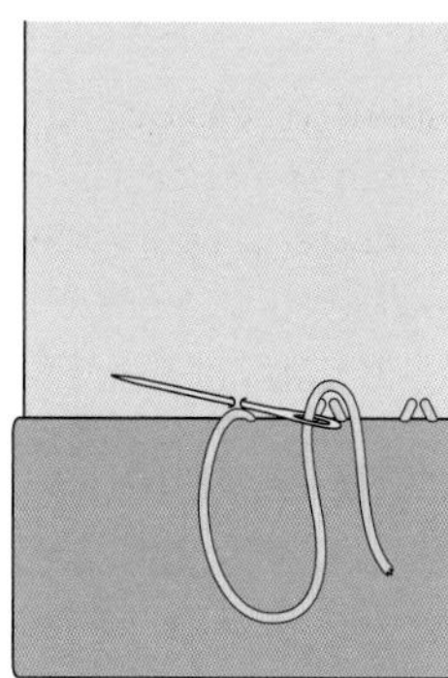

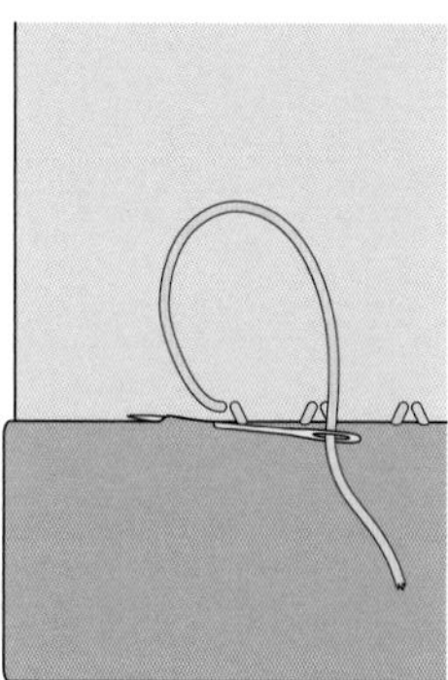

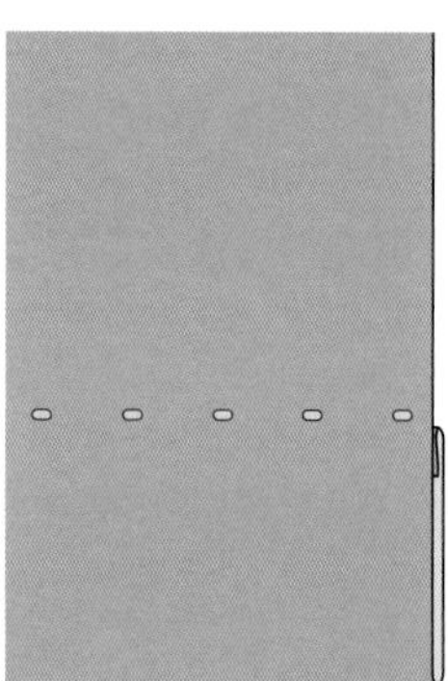

Fig 11

HEM STITCH (*MITUORI-GUKE*)

This neat hem stitch is used for the collars on the hanten jacket and the yogi quilt, for example. Stitch away from the hand holding the needle.

As shown in Fig 11, slide the needle along inside the hem's folded edge, dipping down into the main fabric to pick up a tiny 1⁄16in (1.5mm) stitch, repeating along the edge. Start and finish with a knot and a few stitches on the underside of the fold, in the opposite direction to the way you will sew.

EDGE STITCH (*MIMI-GUKE*)

Traditionally used to sew down the side seams inside unlined kimono, this stitch is used when, to reduce bulk, the hem is folded over only once, as on the table runner and reversible bookmark. Start and finish in the same way as hem stitch (*mituori-guke*).

Make a small stitch through both layers and come back up close to the edge. Then, referring to Fig 12, take another stitch through the edge but swing the needle outwards, as shown – so you know you are not piercing through to the front of the fabric again – then swing the needle in and come back up through the edge fabric, so you make a stitch around ¾in (2cm) long that lies under the edge without piercing the front of the fabric at all. Make another tiny stitch through both layers and repeat.

Another version of *mimi-guke* is sewn to hold the *susofuki* (hem wipe), the little flash of lining fabric seen at the wrist opening and lower body edge on kimono, and which is used on the hanten jacket. For this stitch, take a small stitch in the lining fabric about a scant ¼in (5mm) from the edge, stitching through the lining and seam allowances only, without going through to the outside of the garment, and repeat.

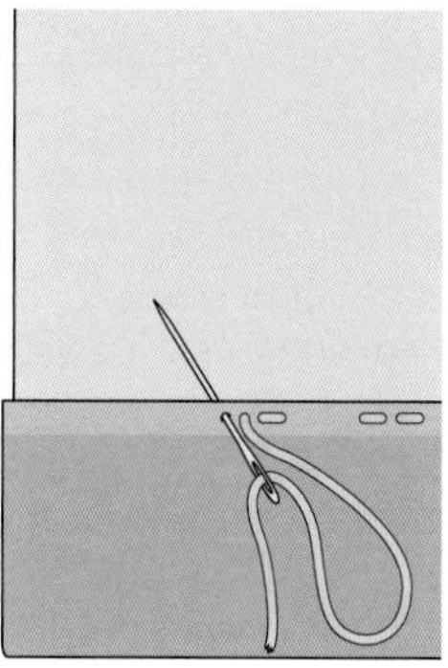

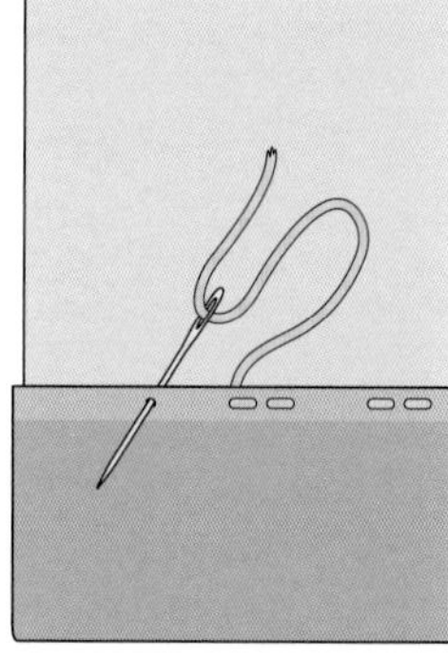

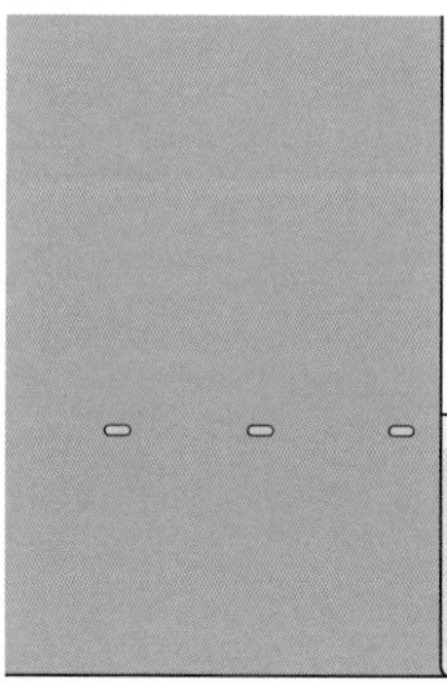

Fig 12

This *mimi-guke* variation holds the lining fabric in place in a *susofuki* (hem wipe) at the hanten jacket hem and wrist opening, for protection and a touch of contrast.

LADDER OR SLIP STITCH (*HASHIGOMATSURI* OR *OKUMATSURE*)

Use this stitch (Fig 13) to close gaps neatly and invisibly, such as the opening on the cushion pad of the box cushion.

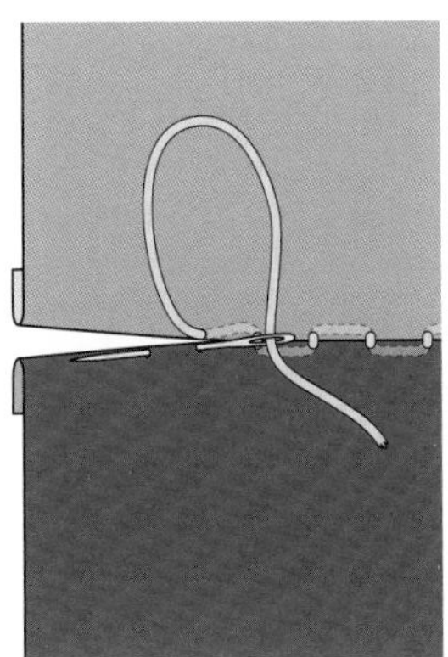

Fig 13

WHIP STITCH (*MAKI-NUI*)

Whip stitch (Fig 14) can be used to finish a raw edge by hand in lieu of a machine-sewn zigzag, as I have done for the box cushion. It has also been used decoratively to finish the machine-sewn seams on the outside of the komebukuro bag, for example, to neaten the raw edges.

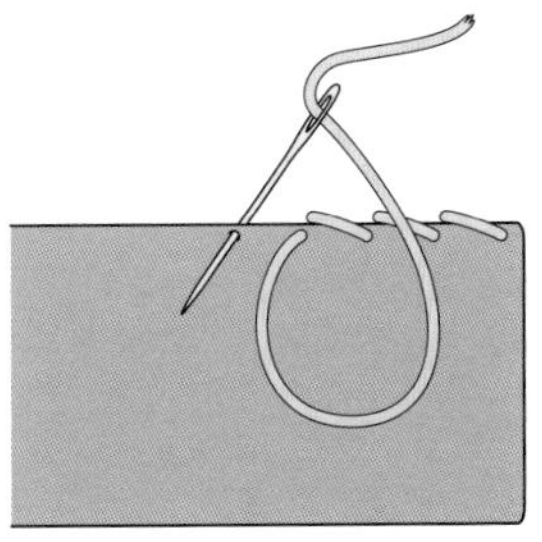

Fig 14

Whip stitch is sewn in both directions for a crossed-over X effect along the seams of the tote bag. For a stronger finish, either stitch with the thread doubled or stitch each row twice, going in and out at the same point for both stitches.

modern boro stitches

Boro-inspired pieces by contemporary stitchers often include utility and embroidery stitches that might not stand up to as much hard use as traditional boro stitches, mainly because they are more three dimensional so prone to wearing through. However, the effect can be very attractive.

BLANKET STITCH

Sew towards your working hand. Blanket stitch (Fig 15) can be used as a decorative stitch or as an edging stitch. For appliqué , it can be sewn over a raw or a turned edge.

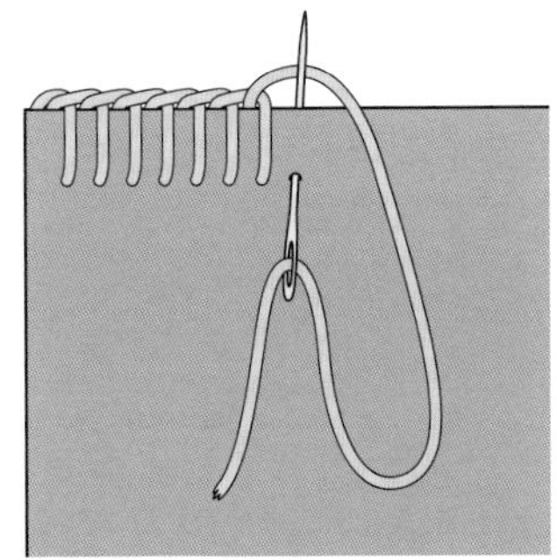

Fig 15

Blanket stitch is used to add interest to some of the reverse appliqué 'holes' in the table runner.

CHAIN STITCH

This stitch is made from a series of loops, so it will unravel if the thread is broken. Stitch from right to left for right-handers (Fig 16), and from left to right for left-handers. Secure the last stitch with a tiny running stitch.

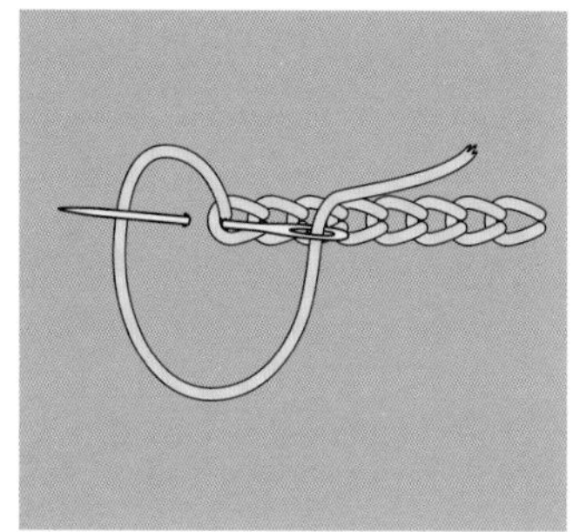

Fig 16

Chain stitch spirals on the table runner give a contemporary boro style, but won't take very hard wear.

SEED STITCH

A series of random running stitches (Fig 17), producing an attractive effect that has the added bonus of being very hard wearing. Keep your stitches short on the back; around ¼in (6mm) long is good.

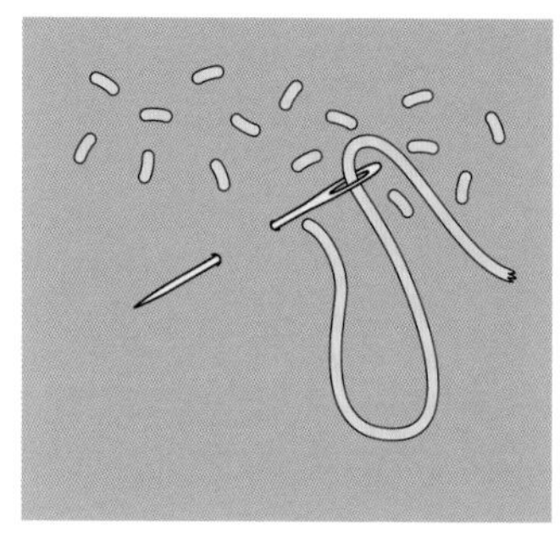

Fig 17

Seed stitch worked on the patched sections of the messenger bag is functional, tough, and looks contemporary.

RANDOM CROSS STITCH

Use this simple stitch to decoratively fill in areas in a similar way to seed stitch. Strand across the back of the fabric, or between layers, to where you want the next cross to be, as shown by the dotted lines between the crosses in Fig 18.

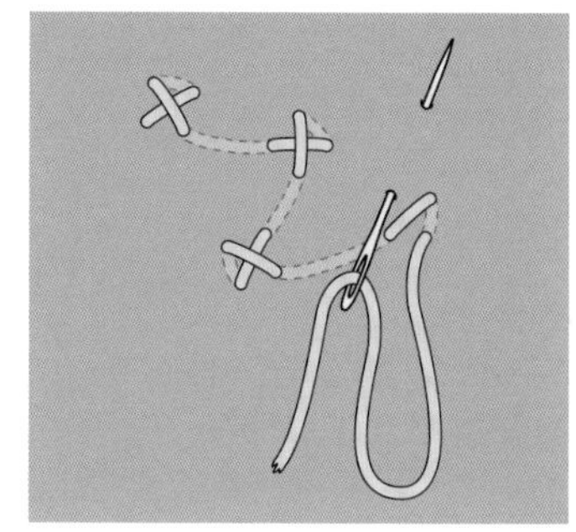

Fig 18

A smattering of random cross stitch suggests tiny stars in the sky on the greetings card miniature.

simple sashiko

Sashiko means 'little stab' or 'little pierce' and this stitching technique, originally used for work clothes and household items, has gained a worldwide popularity over the last twenty years. While the larger, more decorative sashiko patterns such as *asanoha* (hemp leaf) or *shippo* (seven treasures) are not traditionally stitched over boro patching, very simple lines of sashiko were sometimes stitched as part of a piece of boro. Also, pieces of neatly sewn sashiko were repurposed as boro, or a sashiko garment might become worn and patched as boro.

Sashiko was usually stitched with a doubled thread, but also looks effective sewn singly, which is easier to do through several layers. If you want to include more elaborate sashiko patterns in your contemporary boro-inspired work, there are hundreds of patterns to choose from. The selection of simple *hitomezashi* (one-stitch) patterns described here are typical of the few designs originally used for boro. Mark a ¼in (6mm) or slightly smaller grid to use as a guide and leave a small turning loop, like a curved bracket, at the end of each row.

When using a doubled thread for traditional sashiko, the threads need to be about 1yd (1m) long. Thread the needle, smooth down the thread several times and tie a single knot with the ends together (Fig 19). You gather up and ease out the fabric as you stitch (see Traditional Boro Stitches – Running Stitch) so that the two strands lie parallel in the stitch and don't twist up.

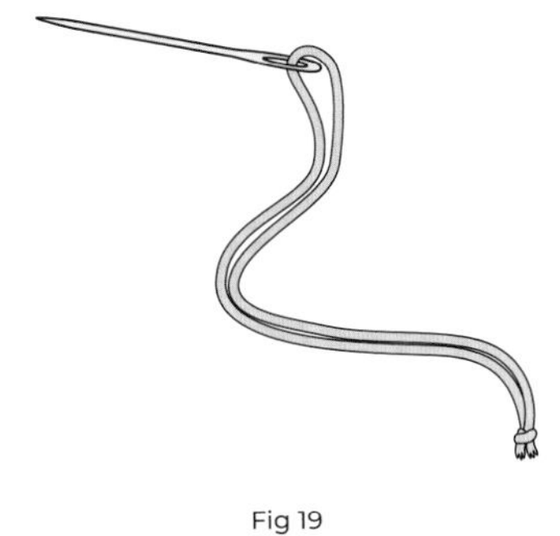

Fig 19

HORIZONTAL ROWS (*YOKOGUSHI*)

This basic stitch forms the first step of many other *hitomezashi* patterns (Fig 20). Stitch back and forth, across the grid, going up and down where the grid lines cross. The position of the stitches and the spaces in between alternate between one row and the next. The stitches should go across one grid square exactly, on the horizontal line. *Yokogushi* is turned through 90 degrees to become vertical lines when it forms the basis of other patterns.

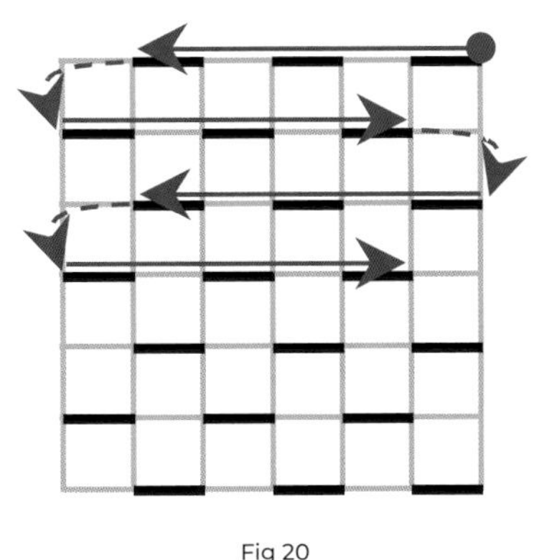

Fig 20

'10' CROSS STITCH (*JŪJIZASHI*)

One of the few patterns in sashiko where the stitches cross, this has a raised texture. Work the first set of stitches as for Horizontal Rows (*yokogushi*). The second set of stitches crosses over the first, at right angles (Fig 21); there is no grid line to guide you for these and you must line them up by eye, from the centre of one square to the next.

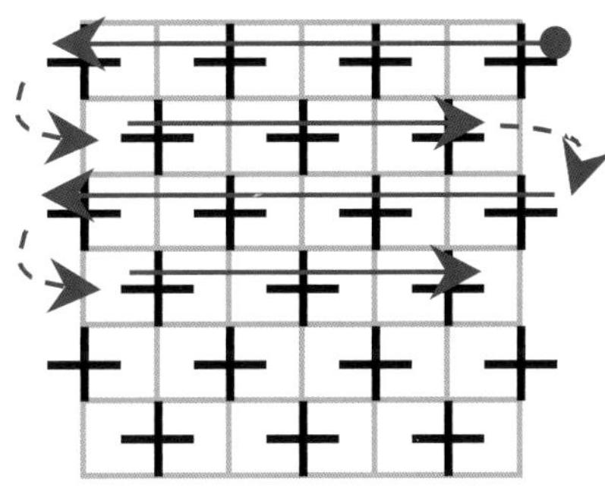

Fig 21

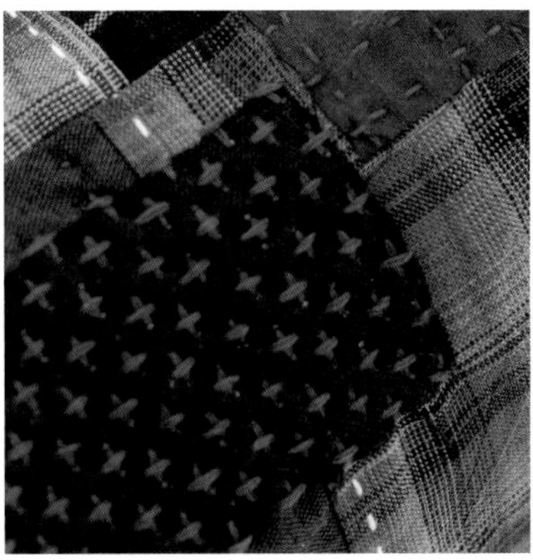

Jūjizashi holds this patch in place on the box cushion project.

PERSIMMON FLOWER STITCH (*KAKINOHANAZASHI*)

Combines alternate rows like Horizontal Rows (*yokogushi*) with pairs of rows that are the same, stitched on a grid as before. The pattern rows in red in the diagrams show these paired rows repeating the previous row. Rows must be in the correct sequence to make the pattern appear, but mistakes can be interesting! Note that the rows have one stitch followed by one gap and there are no double gaps.

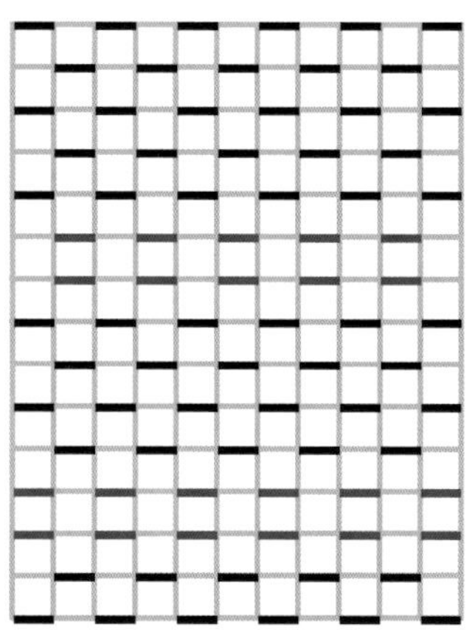

Fig 22a

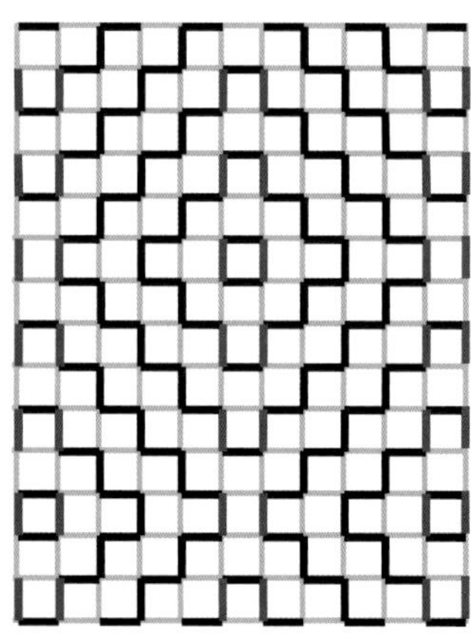

Fig 22b

Pre-printed sashiko fabrics can be stitched separately and appliquéd on, or they can be pinned to your boro and stitched through all the layers together, as was done here on the box cushion. The marking lines will wash out!

wearing in boro

You can speed up the natural ageing process by breaking down the textile. Washing the item on a medium-to-hot wash, for example, will help to 'set' the stitches, making it look used. Toss in some towels at the same time, to slightly abrade the surface.

Scrubbing and rubbing the textile also simulates wear. Think about which areas are likely to become worn most quickly and focus on these. A cheese grater or a surform tool can wear fabrics very quickly. Use scissors to make small cuts here and there. Stonewashing, with gravel in a bucket, is also an option. But don't overdo it – your finished boro still needs to be usable! By far the best way to give boro the patina of age is to use it as much as possible.

making up projects

There are several simple techniques used on more than one project which are included here – a traditional seam finish, boxed-out corner, and a method for finishing flat items that avoids the need for a bound edge. You may find these useful for your own designs too.

KISE FOLD

This is a construction technique seen on the seams of traditional Japanese garments and it has been used on both the hanten jacket and the yogi quilt. Instead of the seam being pressed cleanly to one side, as we would do for patchwork, a little of the top fabric is allowed to fold over the seam stitches, by about 1⁄16in (1–2mm). On traditional kimono, where the seams are handsewn with running stitches, this is necessary to protect the stitching, and it makes a nice detail on machine-sewn seams as well. Fig 23 shows how the *kise* fold looks when viewed along the seam allowance.

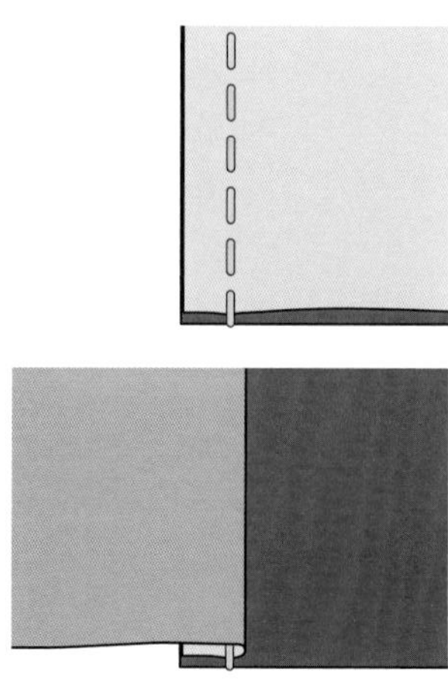

Fig 23

BOXED-OUT CORNERS

Boxing-out corners, on the inside or the outside, is an easy way to make a bag or a cushion more three dimensional without adding a gusset, although you will need to increase the length and width of the piece to compensate (in the project instructions, this calculation has already been done for you). Fold each corner into a point (as shown in Fig 24), either on the inside or the outside depending on the project, and pin in place. Draw a line across the corner at right angles to the seam, measuring from the corner point the distance outlined in the project instructions, and stitch across this line. Following the project instructions, either trim off the excess corner fabric by the amount directed or fold up the triangular flap and stitch it to the side or base of the item.

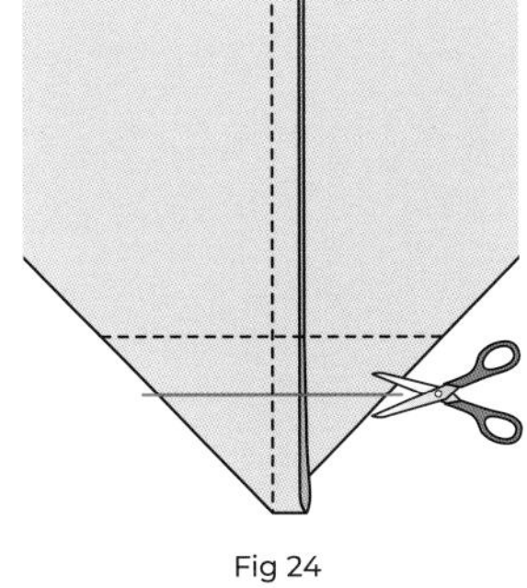

Fig 24

The boxed-out corners on the tote bag are trimmed back quite close to the stitching line, and the raw edges covered with whip stitch by hand.

BUTTED-EDGE FINISH

This gives a neat, flat edge finish, with sharp corners, without a separate binding. On large pieces such as the sofa throw, where two layers of fabric are joined together, first work a line of hand running stitch 1in (2.5cm) from the edge, then start to tuck in ½in (1.3cm) all around the edge, folding the front and back in against each other. At each corner, fold in the seam allowances of the back and front in opposite directions and overlap them before tucking them in (Fig 25). Ladder stitch or slip stitch may be added right at the edge for a neater finish, drawing the edges close together. For smaller items such as the reversible placemat, press ½in (1.3cm) to the back all around the panel before folding it in half to create a front and back. Hand sew running stitch all around the edge, stitching through the four fabric layers.

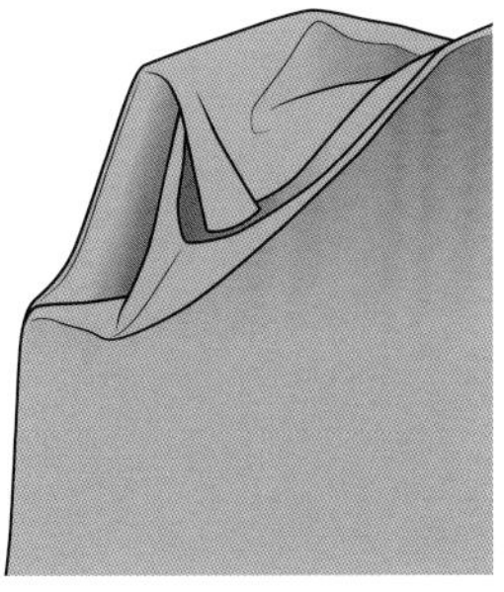

Fig 25

The butted-edge finish makes a neat corner on the sofa throw.

boro on existing clothes

Boro-style repairs on clothes you already have, such as jeans, is often a good first introduction to boro. As denim loses some of its weight when it is worn, patch it with a lighter-weight fabric or with recycled denim. Raw-edge patches can be added from the inside or the outside of the jeans, depending on the desired degree of raggedness. Cream or indigo thread works best. On very narrow jeans, temporarily unpick the leg seam for easier stitching (unpick the seam that doesn't have topstitching detail). For stretch denim, cut fabric on the bias for more stretch and stitch diagonal or curved lines, or stick to vertical lines only. Small boro patches can be added to t-shirts and other stretch fabrics.

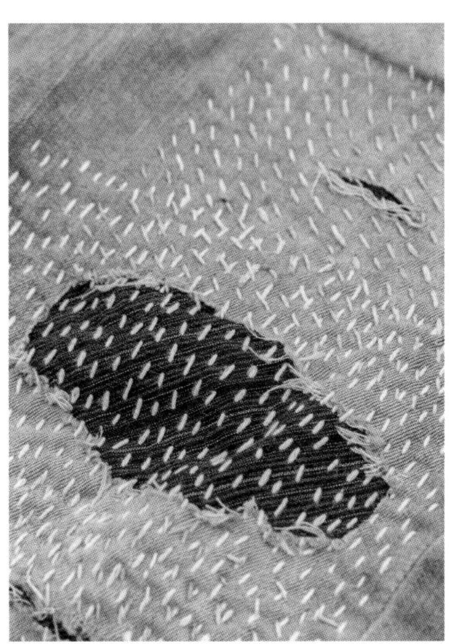

Boro-style jeans repair is a good opportunity to play with different improvisational stitching.

dyeing fabrics and threads

Both fabrics and threads can be dyed easily at home and your options are briefly introduced in this section. Most old boro textiles are indigo. The original colour of your fabrics will affect the finished shade, so you will get greens if yellow is overdyed with blue, while oranges make brownish shades. Harmonious effects can be achieved by dyeing a finished (or partly finished) piece of stitching with a little blue, to tint the fabrics rather than drastically change the colour.

When dyeing your materials, keep bowls or other kitchen utensils solely for that purpose, and never reuse them for food. Work in a well-ventilated space and wear a mask to avoid inhaling the dye powder. Indigo stains everything, so try to do all your indigo dyeing outdoors. You can use natural indigo, synthetic indigo, Procion dye or other chemical dyes.

Natural and synthetic indigo dye share the same process. For your first indigo dyeing session, use an indigo dye kit, which comes with full instructions. Prepare the dye bath in a large container, including adding the chemical supplied to reduce the water's oxygen level. It will be greenish-yellow when ready, with a purplish-blue scum on top, and must be kept warm (around body temperature or a little warmer) or the chemical reaction will stop. Wet the fabric, then dip it gently into the dye bath (do not drip or agitate the dye bath as this will add oxygen). The indigo colour develops with oxidization, so when the fabric is removed from the dye, it is bright green, turning blue as it contacts with oxygen in the air. Darker shades are built up by dipping the fabric multiple times.

Procion dye is perhaps the cleanest option for dyeing. It needs soda ash to fix to any material, and if you treat your fabric with soda ash, rather than mixing with the dye, you can use Procion indoors without staining everything it touches. It can also be stored, mixed with water and ready to use, in jars or bottles, but for safety's sake always label the containers and keep them out of the reach of children.

Dyes sold for re-dyeing jeans are easily used in the washing machine. They tend to stain and you will need to rinse through your washing machine on a very hot wash afterwards. Some can be used in a microwave, in a lidded container, and make shaded effects and shibori tie-dyeing quick and easy. Always check the manufacturer's instructions carefully before use.

Skeins of thread are easy to dye yourself. Tie around the skein loosely several times to stop the threads tangling during dyeing and rinsing. Space-dyed and shaded effects can be achieved by wrapping the thread with rubber bands (cover longer sections with pieces of plastic bag secured with rubber bands) or by placing only part of the thread in the dye bath.

Natural indigo was used to overdye some pieces of recycled linen and also to dye thread with different shading effects.

how to use this book

There are ten project chapters in this book, each including one main project that has been inspired by an original boro item in my collection. Some are traditional, such as the komebukuro bag, the hanten jacket and the yogi quilt – the kind of items that could have been found in any rural Japanese home. Others, such as the messenger bag, the table runner and the tote bag, give a more contemporary application for boro. You can follow the project instructions, adapting sizes to suit your own needs, or use my designs as a starting point for your own ideas. When it comes to changing fabric or thread colours, there are no rules.

The original inspiration for each project is illustrated in Boro History, where you can see a photo or two of the whole item. In the project chapter introduction itself, I have included a detail photo of the vintage boro piece, honing in on what has inspired me, from the texture to the technique.

Each project chapter also includes a 'mini' project, a smaller item based on the main design, providing an opportunity to try out techniques on a much smaller scale. These were inspired by the tradition of *hinagata*, miniature versions of clothing and other household items that were once used to teach girls how to sew. Some of the mini projects are relatively quick makes, ideal for gifts, like the chiku-chiku coaster or reversible bookmark, while others, such as the hinagata hanten or hinagata yogi, will take longer.

Measurements for making the projects are given in imperial first with a metric conversion in brackets. While it is less confusing overall to follow one system or the other throughout, you are not working to the precise tolerances of fine patchwork, and a measurement being out by a tiny fraction isn't going to cause a problem.

Although they often look like doll's clothes or accessories, *hinagata* were 'samplers' for making both clothing and household textiles. This miniature *hinagata yogi* measures around 12in (30.5cm) long, but a full-sized version of these giant kimono-shaped quilts would have been more like 80in (2m) long! *Yogi* range from the most luxurious silks to the most ragged boro. This one is made from printed and plain cottons and dates from the early twentieth century.

projects

tote bag

A simple tote bag for grocery shopping will rapidly become boro as you use it every day. Designed for heavy use, a foundation panel is covered in raw-edge fabric patches, added from what will become the base of the bag and overlapped like roof shingles towards the top, so that crumbs won't get trapped behind. The patches can be old or new, but the fabric chosen for the foundation and the handles needs to be strong. I have machine stitched the narrow side seams and the boxed-out corners at the base, working handsewn whip stitches over the top so that it looks as if the bag has been completely handstitched. It's easy to make the tote bag larger or smaller – just remember that the size will be about half the length of the foundation panel, which is folded in half to make the bag.

my inspiration

This futonji *(futon cover) includes many pieces of* kasuri *(ikat) fabric carefully selected to blend in from the front, but from the back, as seen here, it is a different story, with a riot of different blue and white patches, plus some large pieces of brown printed fabrics in the corner.* Kasuri, *like this large-scale design which alternates a pictorial castle motif with a* tofu *pattern, was handwoven and expensive when new, so worth repairing.*

you will need

- One piece of striped or plain cotton fabric 15 x 39in (38.1 x 99cm), for the bag foundation*
- Two pieces of striped or plain fabric 4½ x 14in (11.4 x 35.6cm), for the handles
- Assorted fabric scraps, approx. 2–4in (5–10.2cm), to include plains and woven patterns, for the patches
- 110yd (100m) fine or medium sashiko thread in medium-cream
- Dark grey or dark blue machine sewing thread
- Basic sewing kit (see Tools and Materials)

**I have used narrow-width striped kimono cotton.*

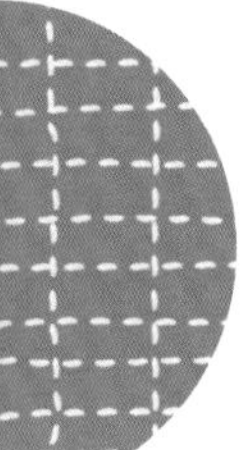

1 **Make the bag handles:** Fold and press each 4½ x 14in (11.5 x 35.5cm) piece of fabric as shown in Fig 1, then use sashiko thread to hand sew running stitch down each long side about 1⁄16in (1.5mm) from the edge, working through all layers. Add another three rows of running stitch evenly spaced down the centre of the handles, for reinforcement.

2 **Prepare the bag foundation panel:** Take your 15 x 39in (38 x 99cm) piece of cotton fabric and fold and press a ½in (1.3cm) hem towards you at each short end. There is no need to stitch this hem in place, as it will be covered with fabric patches and sewn down as you make your boro. I used traditional narrow-width Japanese fabric for this bag's foundation, so that the selvedges were retained on the sides of the panel, but if you are using a piece of cut cotton fabric, you can leave the side edges raw.

3 **Start to add fabric patches to the bag foundation:** Begin to cover the foundation panel with fabric patches roughly in a line across the centre, overlapping the pieces by at least ½in (1.3cm), as shown in Fig 2. This will become the bottom of the bag, so choose the strongest fabrics. Pin the first patches in place.

4 Add more patches, again overlapping the previous ones by at least ½in (1.3cm), as shown in Fig 3. When several patches have been pinned in place, stitch a large rectangular spiral of running stitches to hold them in position, then remove the pins.

5 Continue adding patches, overlapping the previous ones each time as before (do take care not to accidentally cover any pins as you do so), and, after covering another 3–4in (7.6–10.2cm) of foundation fabric, stitch another rectangular spiral to hold them in place. Gradually cover all of the foundation fabric with patches in this way (Fig 4). Vary the size, colour and pattern of your patches to ensure that the front and the back of the finished bag look different. Note that the raw edges of any fabric patches at the sides of the bag will be hidden by the whip-stitched edge when the bag is constructed in step 10.

6 **Attach the bag handles:** Position a bag handle at each end of the foundation fabric on the same side as the boro patches (the ends of the handles are not turned unde,r as these will be covered with more patches in step 7). Make sure the bag handles are centred along the width and that the handle ends overlap the edge of the bag panel by approx. 1in (2.5cm), with a gap between the handle ends of approx. 3½in (8.9cm). Check that the handles are the same length and identically positioned at each end of the bag panel, and that they are not twisted, then sew them in place with several lines of running stitches, going back and forth (Fig 5) or in an X shape.

Fig 1

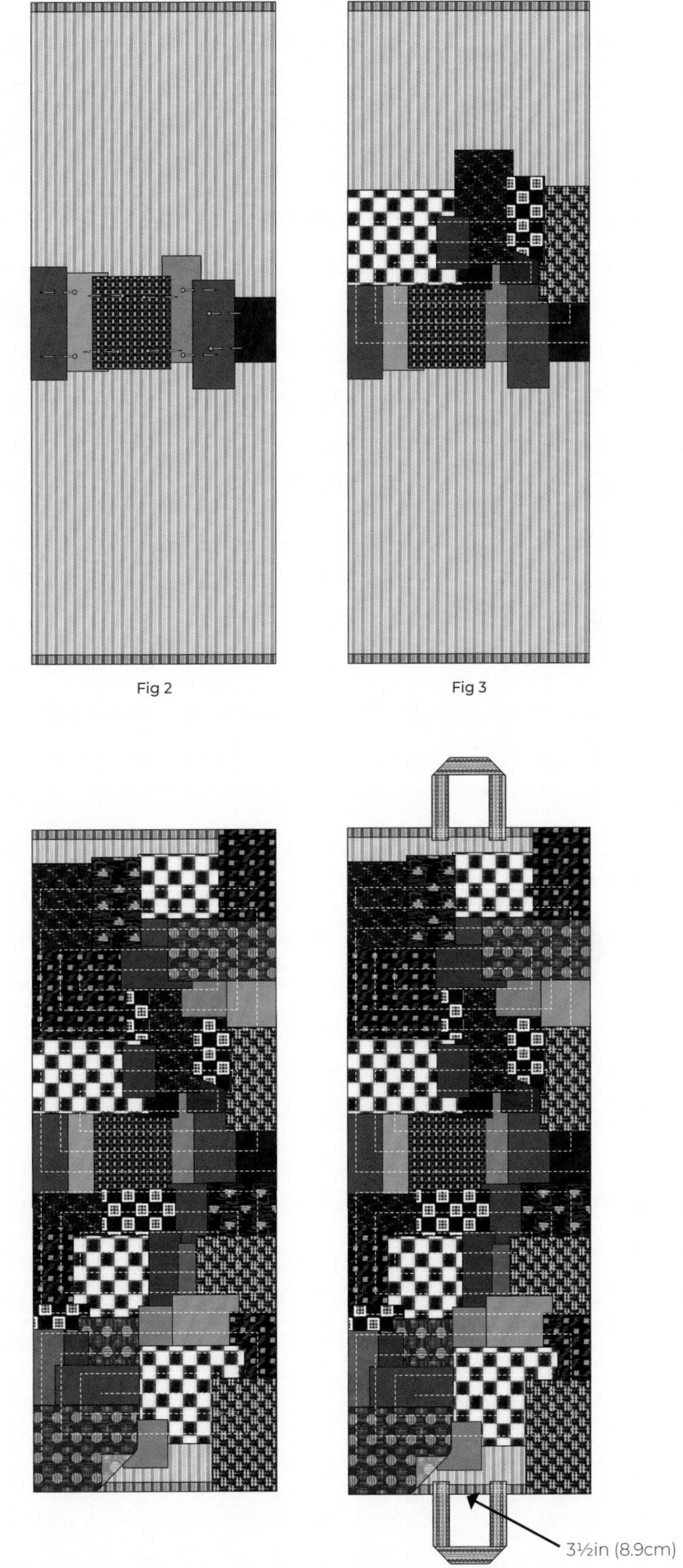

Fig 2

Fig 3

Fig 4

Fig 5

7 Continue to add fabric patches to the bag foundation: Following the instruction in steps 3–5, continue to add fabric patches to each end of the foundation fabric until it is completely covered. When adding the final row of patches, turn under a ½in (1.3cm) hem allowance on each patch where it meets the edge of the foundation panel (unless, of course, you choose to have a raw edge at the top of your bag).

8 When all the patches have been sewn in place, add extra lines of running stitch all over the boro panel, both horizontally and vertically. The lines don't have to go all the way across but they do want to be fairly close together, between ⅜in (1cm) and 1in (2.5cm) apart. Try to stitch over the raw edges of patches whenever possible to prevent fraying.

9 Add lines of reinforcing stitches: Turn the panel over to the unpatched side and sew some extra stitching lines where the base of the bag will be once it has been constructed (i.e. the central area) for extra reinforcement. If you are using striped fabric for the foundation, you could follow the stripes; vary your thread colour if you wish.

10 Construct the bag: Fold the bag panel in half so that the patches are on the outside, line up at the sides and pin in place (the seams will be on the outside of the project). Using dark thread, machine sew the bag sides together about ⅛in (3mm) from the edge, starting and finishing with a few backstitches. Box-out the corners at the base of the bag (see Techniques: Making Up Projects), machine sewing 1in (2.5cm) up from the corner point, then trimming the corner point to leave a ⅛in (3mm) seam allowance.

11 Use sashiko thread to whip stitch by hand, first up, then down the seams for a crisscross effect (see Techniques: Traditional Boro Stitches). For a stronger finish, either use a doubled thread or stitch each row twice, overlapping the stitches neatly, or not, as is your preference. (If this stitching starts to wear out as the bag is used, it can easily be replaced.)

12 Optional finishing technique: Turn the bag inside out and add a small reinforcement patch across the top of the side seams, stitching from the inside. These reinforcements can be as small as 1 x 2in (2.5 x 5cm) and 'bridge' the top of the side seams inside the bag, so that the stitching can't be pulled apart when the bag is very full.

13 'Wear in' the bag: To give the bag a used look, machine wash it at 40–60°C. This will slightly wrinkle the boro and help to 'set' the running stitches.

mini tote bag

The tote bag is easy to make in any size you wish, simply by changing the size of the foundation fabric, and it can easily be adapted to make a much smaller version. The foundation fabric for my mini tote bag is 7½ x 18½in (19 x 47cm), a quarter of the size of the original bag. The foundation fabric could also be pieced from scraps if you prefer, and the straps made from slightly shorter, narrower strips, as the smaller bag will never carry much weight.

Without the box-out base, the mini tote bag is much flatter, making it ideal to carry items such as tablet computers, e-readers or slim paperback books. The finished bag was not washed, so the patches have crisper edges.

sofa throw

A flat piece of boro is a relatively easy thing to make. This throw measures 65 x 50in (165 x 127cm), making it a handy size to snuggle under on the sofa. It is made from two layers of pieced fabric joined with simple sashiko stitching spirals, in red and assorted blue sashiko threads, and it has a butted-edge finish, similar to many old *bodo* (bedding sheets). I have used some Japanese reproduction fabric samples, including some faux patchwork, which makes the piecing look more intricate. A piece from the Tadashi Morita collection, which I saw at the 'Boro, Threads of Life' exhibition (London, 2014), had the same square spiral sashiko carefully stitched, with more patches on top, giving it the appearance of more than one person's handiwork, so I adapted this detail.

my inspiration

This thick bodo *(bedding sheet) has many different cotton fabrics, including several pieces of the same* kasuri *ikat fabric. The back, shown here in detail, a fabulous assortment of fabrics in subdued colour and value, seems to have been constructed mainly in strips, with patches added on top. The other side is more carefully co-ordinated and the stitching is quite unobtrusive. It was made with care. The front of my throw combines features from both sides.*

you will need

- Assorted lengths of cotton fabric, including plains, prints and woven patterns, 10¾in (27.3cm) wide, for the front panel*
- Fabric scraps in various sizes, for added patches
- One pieced panel 67 x 52in (170 x 132cm) or slightly larger, for the backing panel**
- 220yd (200m) fine or medium sashiko thread in dark red and several blue shades
- Dark grey or dark blue machine sewing thread
- Basic sewing kit (see Tools and Materials)
- Ruler, approx. 1¼in (3.25cm) wide

**You will require approx. 2½yd (2.25m) of 43¼in (110cm) wide fabric in total. For further advice, see step 1.*

***The backing panel can be made from any combination of fabric pieces, to measure at least 1in (2.5cm) larger all around than the front panel. For the details of how I made mine, see step 3.*

1 Piece the patchwork strips for the front panel: You will need several strips of patchwork to make the front panel as identified in Fig 1. The throw can be made to any size you wish, either by using narrower or wider fabric pieces to make the patchwork strips or simply by increasing or reducing the number of strips sewn around the central set of three (A–C). It is interesting to note that many old boro pieces started by piecing back together an approximation of the traditional *tan* bolt width (13¾–15in/35–38cm), often from half *tan* widths, but I have used a more economical 10¾in (27.3cm) strip width, which is approximately a quarter of the modern fabric bolt width, as this was the size of all the scrap sample pieces I had.

Sew the 10¾in (27.3cm) wide pieces of fabric, working either by hand or machine, into several strips. You will need four 10¾ x 45¾in (27.3 x 116.2cm) strips – three for the throw centre (A–C), plus one side panel (D); two 10¾ x 40¾in (27.3 x 103.5cm) strips for the top and bottom panels (E and F); and one 10¾ x 65¾in (27.3 x 167cm) strip for the remaining side panel (G). It is easiest to make the strips slightly longer than required, then trim them to fit.

If you are using a very bold fabric, such as the red faux *kasuri* (ikat) dot print that I have used, it will look better if you cut it up and have the fabric in several places around the patchwork. My choice of faux patchwork fabrics has helped to make the piecing look more elaborate, but you could sew some sections from smaller pieces of fabric for a similar effect. Try sewing pieces together in pairs and placing these until you are happy with the arrangement.

Use ⅜in (1cm) seam allowances throughout and press each seam to one side. If hand sewing, small running stitches are fine, as none of the seams will be cut through after stitching.

Fig 1

Fig 2

2 Join the patchwork strips to make the front panel: Working either by machine or by hand, first pin, then sew the four 10¾ x 45¾in (27.3 x 116.2cm) strips together in pairs. Then pin and sew the two pairs together to give you a squarish patchwork panel, pressing the seams to one side. Now sew one of the 10¾ x 40¾in (27.3 x 103.5cm) strips across the top of the patchwork panel and one across the bottom, pressing the seams towards the outside. Finally, to complete the front panel (Fig 2), sew the 10¾ x 65¾in (27.3 x 167cm) strip to the right-hand side, again pressing the seam outwards.

3 Piece the backing panel: I made the backing panel by sewing together three 43¼in (110cm) wide cotton prints measuring 28½in (72.4cm), 17½in (44.5cm) and 22½in (57.2cm), with an additional 8¼ x 67in (21 x 170cm) strip (pieced from two lengths of the same fabric) sewn down one side. Press the seams to one side.

Throw back view. The square spiral stitching creates secondary patterns across the larger patchwork pieces.

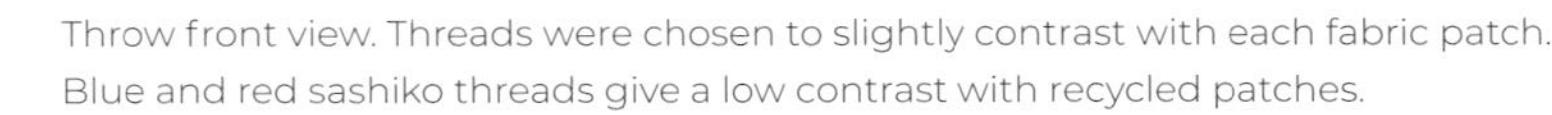

Throw front view. Threads were chosen to slightly contrast with each fabric patch. Blue and red sashiko threads give a low contrast with recycled patches.

Fig 3

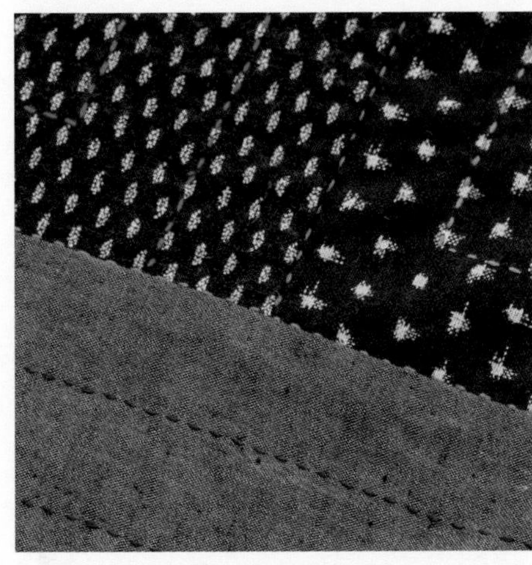

4 Layer up the top and backing panels: Lay the backing panel wrong side up and smooth it out. Lay the top panel right side up on top, making sure it is centred – there should be approx. 1in (2.5cm) of the backing panel showing all around. Pin and then tack (baste) the two layers together, working from the centre outwards and making sure that the straight lines in the piecing are fairly straight. Tack (baste) radiating out from the centre, as shown in Fig 3, then add extra vertical and horizontal tacking (basting) lines approx. 4in (10.2cm) apart, leaving approx. 1½in (3.4cm) unstitched all around the edge so that you can turn them in to make a hem in step 5.

5 Hem the throw: Trim the backing panel to match the top panel exactly. Draw a line all around the throw approx. 1in (2.5cm) from the edge, and hand sew running stitch through both layers, using a single thread of blue sashiko thread. Turn the edges inwards by ½in (1.3cm) evenly all round and pin in place. Following the instructions for the butted-edge finish (see Techniques: Making Up Projects), ladder stitch around the edge of the throw, tucking the corners in as you go. For a neat, firm edge, work an extra row of sashiko-style running stich about ⅛in (3mm) from the edge all round.

6 Stitch the layers together: Using a single thread of blue sashiko thread, stitch the two layers together 'in the ditch', i.e. hand stitch running stitch as close as possible along all the patchwork seams, on the opposite side from where the seam allowance has been pressed each time, so the stitches are right against the slight bump of the seam, as shown in the detail photo. Stitch the longest continuous lines first, i.e. between the long strips, then stitch the shorter lines, including any faux patchwork seams.

7 Mark and stitch the square spirals: Working in each patch in turn, use a 1¼in (3.25cm) wide ruler to draw a vertical line down the left-hand side of the patch, then across the bottom and up the right-hand side, continuing to mark the spiral to the centre of the patch; the centre of the spirals can be finished in various ways, depending on the proportions of the patch and the effect you want (see photo details). Smaller patches and narrower strips, as made by the faux patchwork fabrics, can be marked with a rectangle or just a line through the centre. Use a single sashiko thread to hand sew running stitch along the marked lines through both layers of the fabric, choosing a thread colour that slightly contrasts with the fabric so that the stitching can be seen. Work the square spirals from the top left towards the centre of the spiral.

8 'Wear in' the throw and add extra patches: To give the throw a used look, machine wash it at 40–60°C. This will slightly wrinkle the boro and help to 'set' the running stitches. Once dry, use the various recycled fabric scraps to hand sew extra patches to both the front and the back of the throw. I used slightly worn, recycled fabrics, which were a little thinner than the patchwork fabrics, and turned the edges under all around. Add patches to help balance out the main pieced pattern.

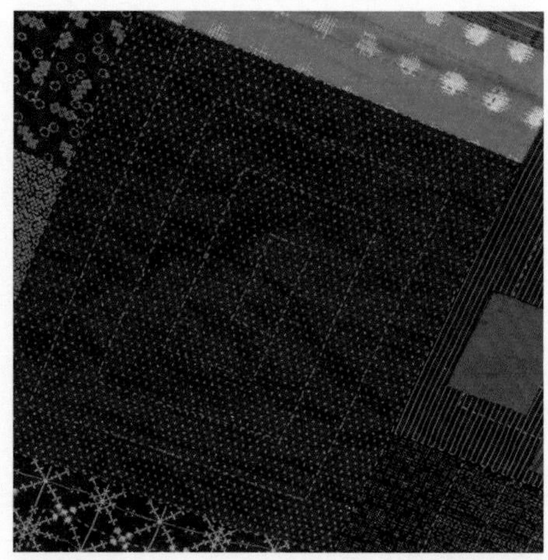

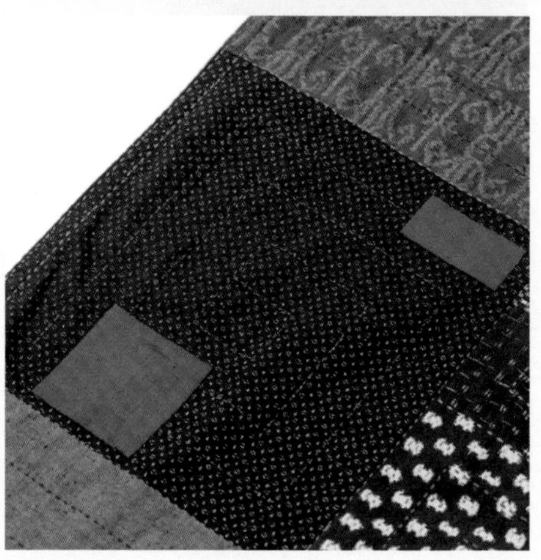

cushion cover

This cushion cover has random patchwork strips bordering a striking central print. The front is made 1in (2.5cm) larger than the pad – this one was 19in (48.3cm) square. Just add strips round the central print until is is large enough. Machine zigzag the seam allowances and add topstitch details. Finish with a simple envelope back made from two rectangles of fabric, cut each to about two-thirds of the width of the front panel. Sew a narrow hem on each backing piece, then place right sides together with the front panel, overlapping the hemmed edges, and stitch all around the outside edge with a ⅜in (1cm) seam allowance (Fig 4). Clip the corners, turn right side out and insert the cushion pad.

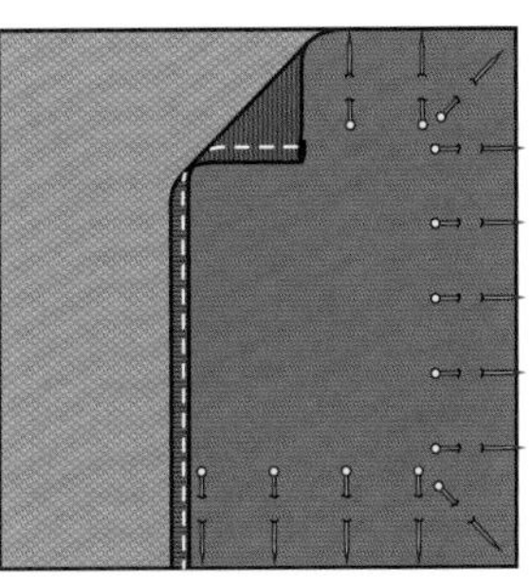

Fig 4

komebukuro bag

Komebukuro were originally used for storing and gifting rice, but these drawstring bags make handy containers for all kinds of things, including threads and fabrics. Traditionally made from scraps, often patchworked from strips of fabric, they have a square base, with the sides forming a cross shape before being sewn together. My heavily patched boro version is constructed slightly differently from an original komebukuro as I have used two strips of new fabric crossed to form the bag shape for the boro foundation, and this means that there is an extra reinforcing layer of fabric in the base. Recycled raw-edge patches are added from the centre of the base outwards and held in place with multiple rows of running stitch, worked with a fine pink sashiko thread to complement my choice of foundation fabric. The side seams are machine sewn and finished with a handsewn whip stitch.

my inspiration

Large random patches cover the inside of this old noragi *work jacket, all indigo dyed in different shades. The bold blocks of colour suggest abstract art and show how subtle different shades of similar colours can look. I used the same colour-block idea for my bag but with much smaller patches, while increasing the variety of fabric colours used.*

you will need

- Two pieces of striped or plain cotton fabric 7½ x 18½in (19 x 47cm), for the bag foundation/lining
- Eight pieces of striped or plain cotton fabric 3½ x 1¾in (8.9 x 4.4cm), for the drawstring loops
- Assorted fabric scraps, approx. 1½–3in (3.8cm–7.6cm) in various dark colours as well as some bright reds, light blues and maroons, including stripes, for the boro*
- Two 3in (7.6cm) circles from scrap fabric, for the drawstring bobbles
- A little wadding (batting) or cotton wool
- Two 32in (81cm) long drawstring cords
- Approx. 54¼yd (50m) fine sashiko thread to co-ordinate with your choice of foundation/lining fabric
- Machine sewing thread
- Basic sewing kit (see Tools and Materials)

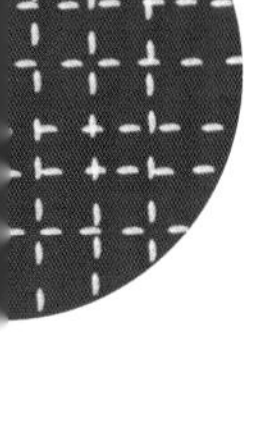

**Your fabric scraps can be square or rectangular – vary the scraps for more interest.*

1 Make the bag foundation: Fold each of the two bag foundation pieces into quarters, folding them in half lengthwise and then in half the other way; crease the fabric and open out again. Lay one piece on top of the other to form a cross, using the creases to help line up the centre base, and pin the layers together. Hand sew running stitch in a square around the bag base and diagonally from corner to corner, as shown in Fig 1, sewing the pieces together.

2 Start to add fabric patches to the bag foundation: Pin the first patch to the centre of the bag base (Fig 2). Add more patches, working outwards from the centre and overlapping the edges by at least ½in (1.3cm) (Fig 3). When several patches have been pinned in place, stitch a square spiral of running stitches to hold them in place, then remove the pins (Fig 4). Continue adding more patches to cover the sides of the bag. Leave approx. 2in (5cm) uncovered at the top edges of the bag panel – this will be covered with patches after the drawstring loops have been added in step 4.

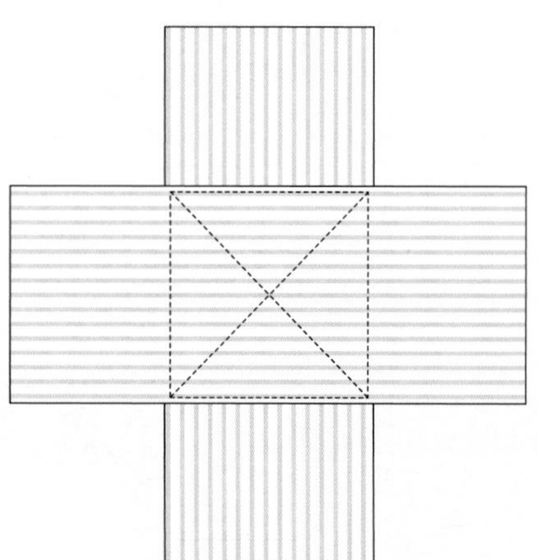

Fig 1

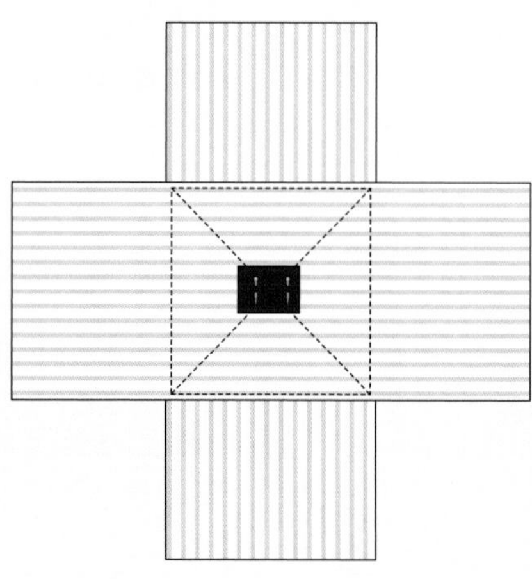

Fig 2

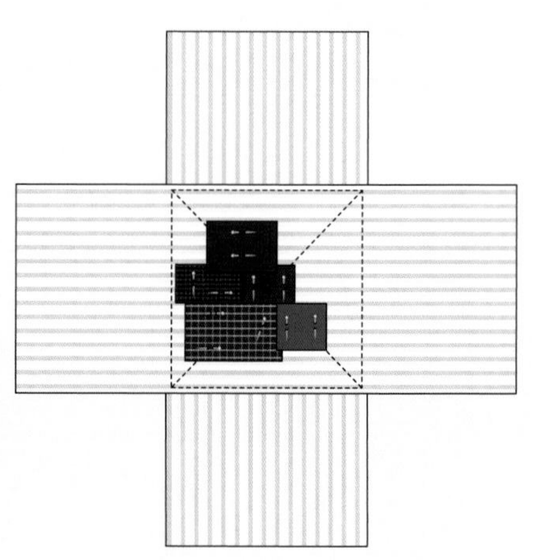

Fig 3

3 Prepare and attach the drawstring loops: Fold and press each 3½ x 1¾in (8.9 x 4.4cm) piece of fabric as shown in Fig 5, then use sashiko thread to hand sew running stitch down each long side of the folded fabric pieces, through all layers, and again along the centre line.

4 Two drawstring loops are attached to the end of each arm of the cross. First, fold the foundation fabric over by ½in (1.3cm) to the outside of the bag (i.e. the side with the patches) and press in place. Find the centre of the folded edge, measure 1½in (3.8cm) to each side of this point, and place a pin to mark the position of each loop. Take one of the prepared pieces and fold it in half to form the loop. Pin in place as marked on the edge of the bag, so that the raw edges overlap the folded edge by approx. ¾in (2cm). Hand stitch in place, sewing through all the layers in an X-shape, which will be quite tough to stitch! Repeat to attach all eight loops (Fig 6).

5 Continue to add fabric patches to the bag foundation: Following the instructions in step 2, continue to add fabric patches to each arm of the cross until they are completely covered. You can leave edges raw at the sides of each arm as these will be sewn into the side seams of the bag, but at the ends (which will become the top edge of the finished bag), turn under the raw edges of the fabric patches by ⅜–½in (1–1.3cm) and overlap the ends of the drawstring loops. Stitch several rows of running stitch along these edges.

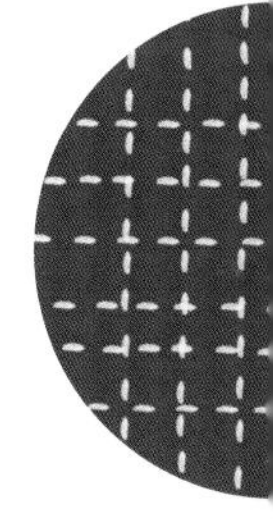

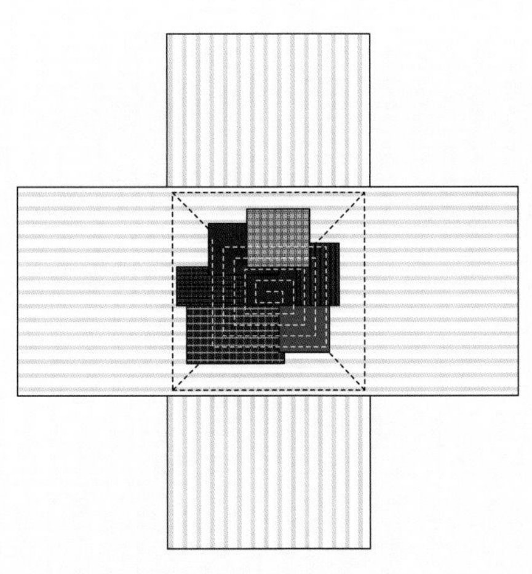

Fig 4

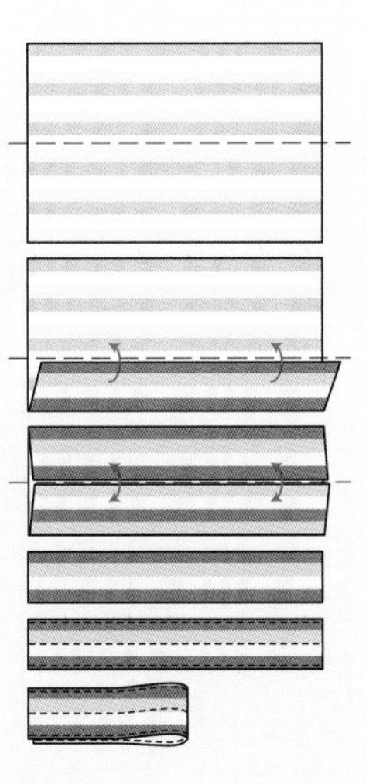

Fig 5

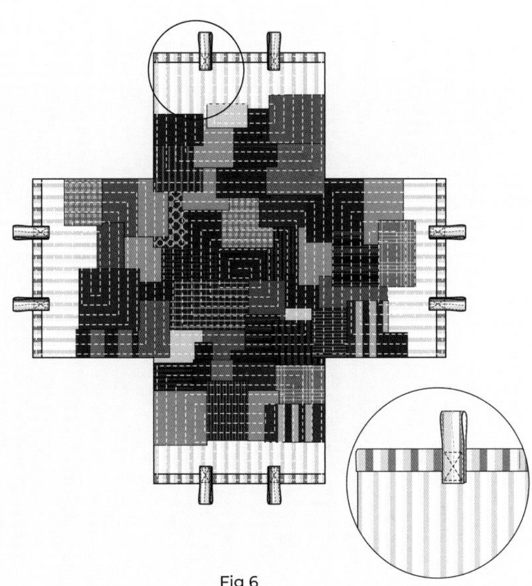

Fig 6

6 When all the patches have been sewn in place, work more rows of running stitch horizontally and vertically across the bag foundation, crossing over the base section. This stitching can become quite dense. Try to stitch over the raw edges of patches whenever possible to prevent fraying (see Techniques: Making Boro-Inspired Textiles).

7 Sew the side seams: Pin each seam in turn and machine sew ⅛in (3mm) from the edge, making sure that the top edge of the bag is lined up neatly from one side to the next. When all the side seams have been machine sewn, use sashiko thread to whip stitch by hand, first up, then down each seam for a crisscross effect.

8 Thread the drawstring cords: Starting and finishing at the middle of one side, thread one of the drawstring cords through all the loops and tie the ends together with a single knot. Starting and finishing at the middle of the opposite side, thread the second drawstring cord through all loops and secure the ends as before.

9 Make the drawstring bobbles: Stitch a gathering thread around each of the two 3in (7.6cm) fabric circles, turning under ¼in (6mm) as you go. Wrap a little bit of wadding (batting) or cotton wool around one of the drawstring knots. Pull up the threads on one of the prepared circles to form a bobble, slip it over the drawstring knot, then pull the thread tightly and secure the bobble with a few stitches through the cord ends. Repeat to cover the end of the remaining drawstring cord.

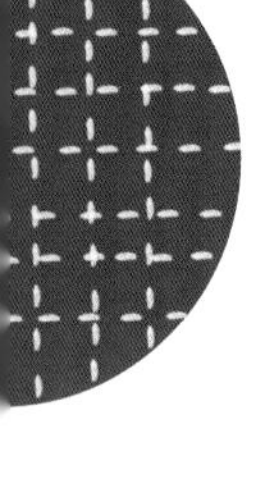

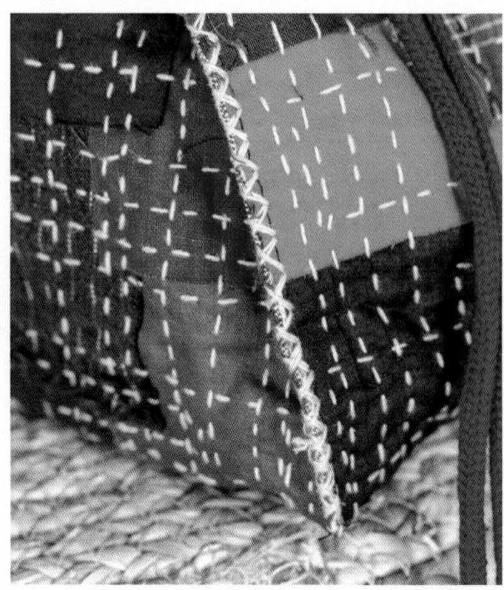

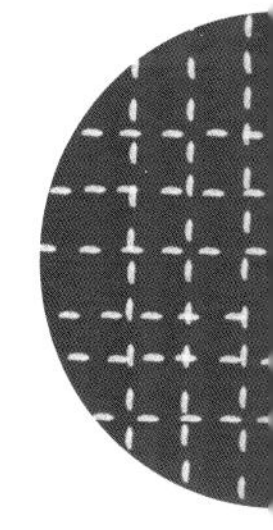

mini komebukuro bag

For this small-scale komebukuro bag, I have used a similar construction style to original komebukuro (see Boro History). The patchwork panels that form the sides are pieced in strips, with the addition of a few raw-edge appliqué patches. Using ¼in (6mm) seams throughout, make a 4½in (11.4cm) pieced square from four 4½ x 1½in (11.4 x 3.8cm) strips. Make four pieced squares in all (the bag side panels), add some raw-edge appliqué patches at random, and sew each to a 4½in (11.4cm) fabric square (the bag base) to make the cross shape that completes the bag outer. Join five 4½in (11.4cm) fabric squares to make the bag lining in the same way. Sew the side seams of the bag outer with right sides together, so that this time the seams are on the inside of the finished bag rather than on the outside as on the larger komebukuro bag. Repeat for the bag lining. Make four drawstring loops (see Komebukuro Bag, step 3) and sew one to the centre of each top side of the lining, with the lining fabric folded over to the outside of the bag by ½in (1.3cm). Fold the top of the bag outer over by ½in (1.3cm), and do the same with the lining. Place the lining inside the bag, wrong sides together, and hand sew all the way around the top. Add drawstring cords (see Komebukuro Bag, step 8).

reversible placemat

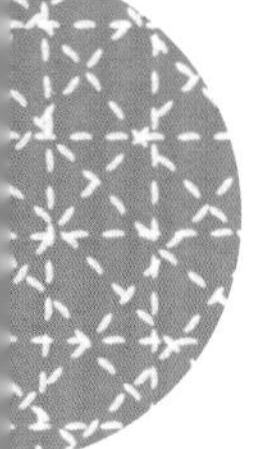

This easy-to-make placemat is created from a single piece of boro-style patchwork, which is then folded in half and held in place with a simple version of the butted-edge finish, as taught to me by Akiko Ike, a contemporary boro textile designer from Niigata City. The layers are stitched together in a sashiko grid pattern and, for an authentic look, the placemat has been distressed to achieve very worn textures. Raw-edge patches have been applied, too, although I have made sure to keep the thickness fairly even across both sides to avoid rocking tableware! The finished placemat measures 9 x 12in (22.9 x 30.5cm), so it is generously sized for soup bowls and small plates, but it can be easily adapted to suit your needs – just decide on the finished size you want, double it, then add a ½in (1.3cm) hem allowance all around.

my inspiration

This small bodoko *has several large plain indigo patches, two on one side and a single patch on the other, all showing different degrees of wear. The origin is unknown, as it was found in a bundle of recycled fabrics bought at a Japanese flea market.*

you will need

- Large fabric scraps, including stripes and checks, equivalent to approx. one fat quarter in area*
- 55yd (50m) medium sashiko threads in cream, blue and tan
- Basic sewing kit (see Tools and Materials)

**Fabrics can be new or recycled. Try including some checked fabrics for a more authentic effect.*

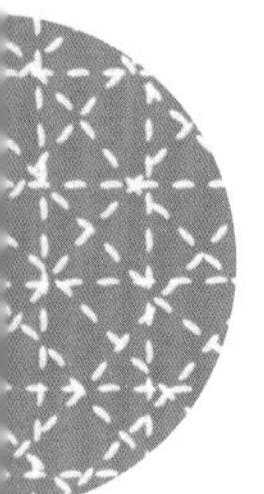

1 Make the patchwork panel: Sew scraps together to make a patchwork panel measuring 19 x 13in (48.3 x 33cm). Select the stronger fabrics for this step. Start by stitching pieces of a similar size together in strips as shown in Fig 1, then sew the strips together to make the panel as shown in Fig 2, using a ⅜in (1cm) seam allowance throughout. Press the seams to one side. It is easier to make the panel slightly larger and trim it to size*. Try to make the patchwork asymmetrical, to avoid seams lining up at the edge when it is folded in half.

**The patchwork can be stitched either by machine or by hand running stitch, but if you are hand stitching, do use backstitch towards the ends of the seams as hand running stitches will unravel when cut through.*

2 Construct the placemat with a butted-edge finish: Fold and press ½in (1.3cm) hem allowances to the wrong side of the patchwork panel, first along one of the short sides (Fig 3a), then along both long sides (Fig 3b), and finally, along the remaining short side (Fig 3c). This ensures that the corners are pressed in opposite directions so that they will tuck in together easily when the panel is folded in half.

3 Fold the patchwork panel in half with wrong sides together, line up the edges and press along the fold line. Tuck in the folded fabric edges at one corner (see Techniques: Making Up Projects), then pin in place and continue to pin along the edge, towards where the panel is folded in half. Tuck in the corner and pin the edge on the opposite side in exactly the same way.

4 Hand sew sashiko running stitch around the edge of the placemat: Thread your needle with a long cream sashiko thread and stitch with the thread doubled if you can (see Techniques: Simple Sashiko). Do not knot the thread tail ends but tuck them inside the panel as shown in Fig 4, and start stitching at the corner with a small, tight backstitch, going through all the corner layers. (There are six layers of fabric at the corner, so you will probably need a thimble to push through this first stitch.) Sew a sashiko running stitch a scant ⅛in (2–3mm) from the edge of the placemat, piercing the tucked-in thread tails. This stitching is all that will hold the edge in place, so do not make the stitches, or the gaps between stitches, too long – a scant ¼in (5–6mm) will be fine. Make sure the stitches are eased out well along the edge and that the fabric is quite flat when you are finished. Stitch all the way around the placemat (Fig 5), making a small backstitch at each corner. When you run out of thread, use the knotless technique to rejoin your thread (see Techniques: Stitching Boro).

5 Mark and stitch the sashiko pattern: Mark a 1½in (3.8cm) grid all over one side of the placemat, as shown Fig 6. Using a doubled thread, sashiko stitch each line of the grid individually, starting and finishing with several stitches in the opposite direction and burying the thread tails between the fabric layers.

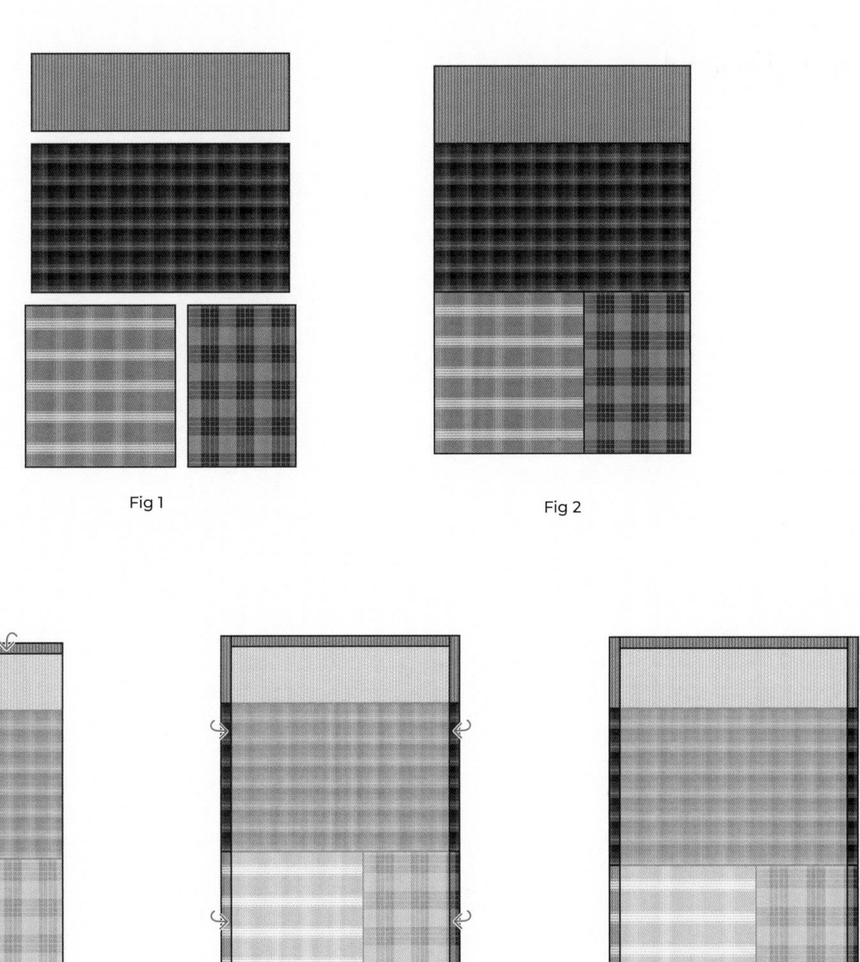

Fig 1

Fig 2

Fig 3a

Fig 3b

Fig 3c

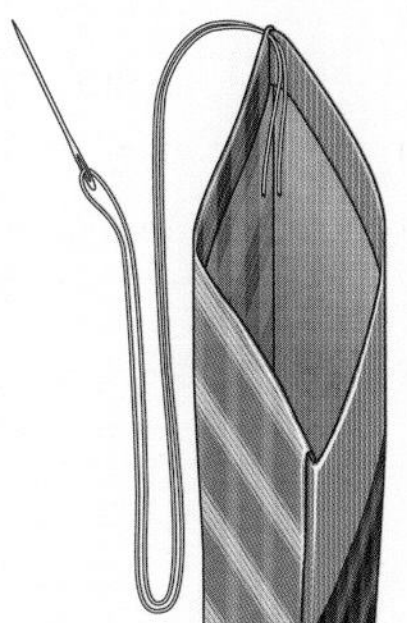

Fig 4

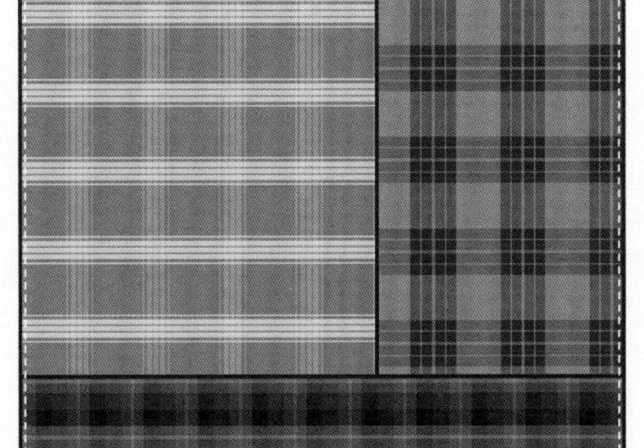

Fig 5

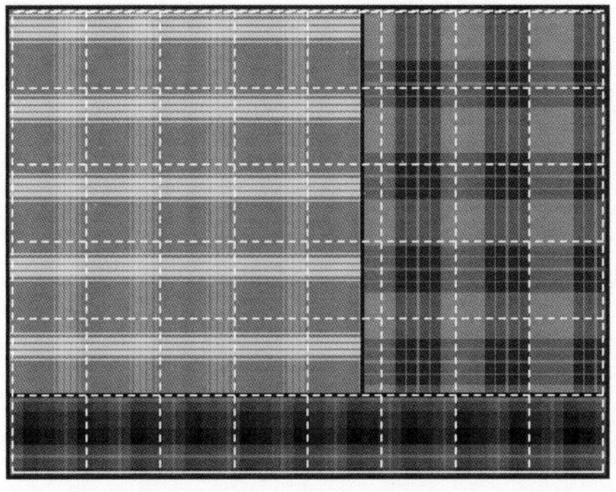

Fig 6

6 Now mark diagonal lines over the stitched grid pattern, as shown in Fig 7. Using a doubled thread, sashiko stitch the diagonal lines. These can be stitched more continuously, starting with one diagonal line and continuing on to the next where it touches the edge of the placemat in a V-formation. I saw this sashiko design on an old *kotatsugake* (heated table cover), where the stitches sometimes crossed in the pattern. Usually in sashiko, you would avoid any stitches crossing over each other, but the occasional crossing of stitches where the pattern lines intersect looks more authentic in this instance.

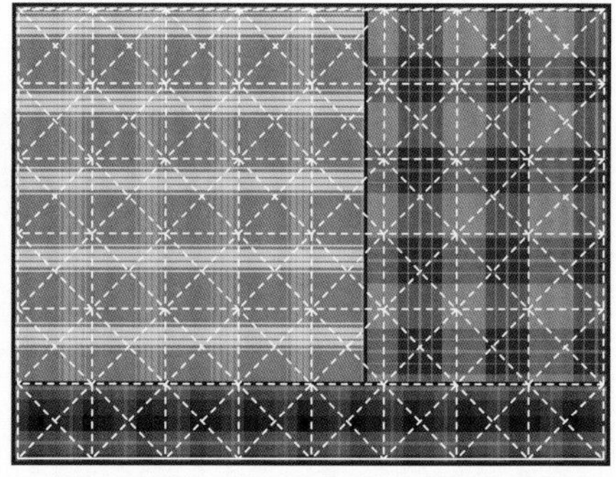

Fig 7

7 Add boro wear effects (optional): Part of the charm of the original piece is the amount of wear it shows, so experiment to give your placemat a similar look. First, machine wash the placemat at 40–60°C. This will slightly wrinkle the boro and help to 'set' the running stitches. I nicked the surface slightly with pointed embroidery scissors before washing. If you accidentally overdo the breakdown, you can always hide the areas you don't like with the raw-edge patches in step 8.

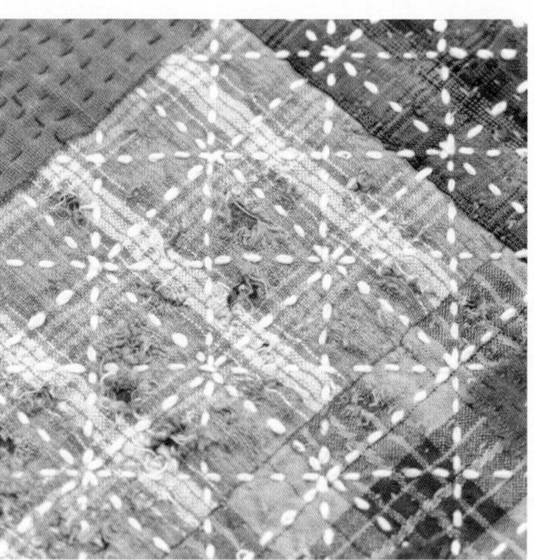

8 Add raw-edge patches: Select some large fabric patches and arrange them on one side (the front) of the placemat asymmetrically. I have left the edges raw for a more ragged effect, but you can turn the edges under if you prefer. Pin the patches in place. Using a single blue sashiko thread, stitch lines back and forth across the patches, approx. ¾in (2cm) apart or slightly closer if you wish. Lines can be marked or stitched freehand, depending on your preference. If you are making a set of placemats, vary the position of the patches on each one.

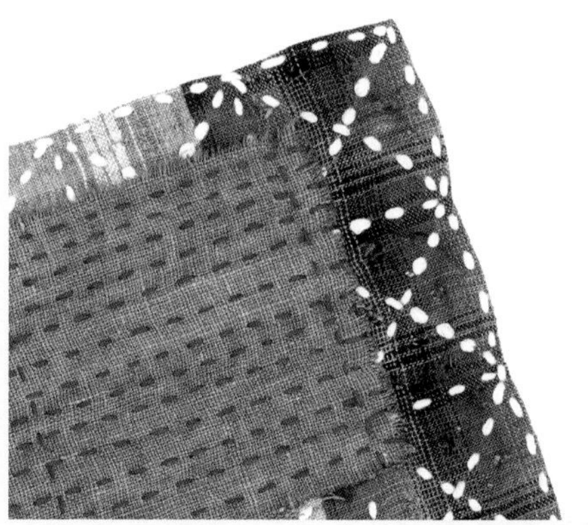

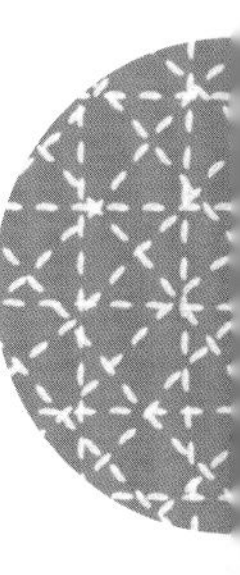

9 Now choose some large patches for the other side (the back) of the placemat and repeat step 8, this time stitching with a single tan sashiko thread, so the stitches will be less obvious than on the front side. To keep the fabric layers even across the mat, you can position some of these patches in areas where the opposite side is less patched.

10 Finishing your placemat with boro texture: To fray broken-down areas and the raw edges of your applied fabric patches a little more, you may want to wash the finished piece once again. Clip off any very long, unravelled threads before using your placemat.

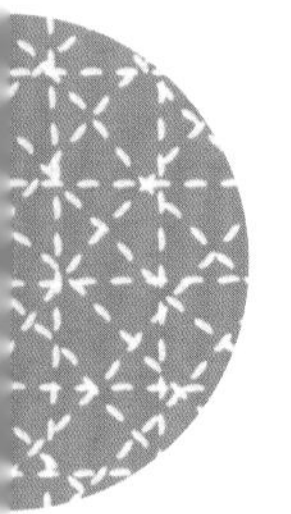

On the side with mainly lighter plaid fabrics, the contrast with the blue patches is more pronounced.

On the other side, the same recycled blue fabric was used for the patches once again, but this time the more faded side is uppermost, which gives a more subtle effect.

chiku-chiku coaster

This miniaturized version of the placemat was inspired by Akiko Ike's 'chiku-chiku' work (see Boro History: Boro Today). Each year she makes a beautiful group cloth by stitching together with herringbone stitch small pieces like these made by visitors to her workshop. I continued this tradition and made these pieces with my sashiko students. To make the coaster, use a rectangular piece of fabric roughly twice as long as it is wide: I used a very thick soft cotton fabric strip measuring approx. 9 x 5in (22.9 x 12.7cm) for a finished size of 4in (10.2cm) square (for a longer mug rug, you'll need to use a squarish rectangle, around a third longer than it is wide). Press and sew the edges in the same way as the table placemat. The rest of the stitching can be as simple or as complex as you like. A square spiral looks good for a quick make. The larger mat seen here was made by stitching several coaster-sized pieces together using herringbone stitch.

mount fuji picture

Almost any fabric scraps can be used to create a simple abstract landscape. Mount Fuji glimpsed by moonlight across Lake Ashi is the quintessential Japanese scene, but you could base your picture on your own favourite panorama. For my stylized view, I have used a piece of new fabric, cut slightly larger than the frame, for the foundation, and I have built up the landscape with recycled raw-edge strips, stitched with oddments of sashiko thread, to suggest lakeside grasses, water ripples and snow. The moon is stitched in a tight running-stitch spiral. This picture is the perfect way to explore boro techniques on a small piece while using up all your thin fabric strips!

my inspiration

The back of this boro panel, probably part of a futon cover, mixes up various piecing, patching and darning techniques, and I find this to be much more interesting than the front of the panel, which is quite co-ordinated. The fabric assortment made me think of how stripes and checks might be used to create landscape effects in a picture or even a map.

you will need

- Picture frame, 9in (23cm) square*
- One piece of fabric 9½in (24cm) square, for the foundation/sky
- One piece of darker fabric approx. 5 x 2½in (12.7 x 6.6cm), for Mount Fuji
- One strip of dark striped fabric approx. 7 x 2½in (17.8 x 6.6cm) with stripes parallel to the long edge, for the hills
- Three strips of assorted plain dark blues approx. 10 x 2½in (25.4 x 6.6cm), for the hills
- Two strips of different stripe, plaid or kasuri ikat fabrics approx. 10 x 2in (25.4 x 5cm) with stripes parallel to the short edge, for the forest and lakeside rushes
- One piece of light blue fabric, approx. 9½ x 2½in (24 x 6.6cm), for the lake
- Sashiko thread oddments in white, cream, dark blue and blue-and-white variegated
- Double-sided adhesive tape to mount the finished picture
- Basic sewing kit (see Tools and Materials)

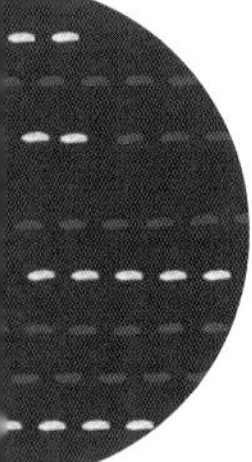

**You can choose any frame size you prefer and adjust your fabric requirements accordingly. Your foundation fabric needs to be at least ½in (1.3cm) larger than the frame size all round.*

1 Fold and position Mount Fuji: Fold the Mount Fuji fabric as shown in Fig 1 and finger press the folds. Referring to the photos of the finished picture, position Mount Fuji (folded side facing down) towards the top of the foundation fabric and slightly to the left (see Fig 2a). Make sure that there is enough room to add the moon later, but don't place the mountain so low that there is insufficient space for the lake fabric at the bottom. Pin the mountain to the foundation, then appliqué stitch along the sloping sides using dark blue sashiko thread.

2 Layer the landscape fabric strips: Now that Mount Fuji has been placed, you can start to layer the raw-edge fabric strips that represent the hills, forest and lakeside rushes. Begin with the strip that has stripes parallel to the long edge (see Fig 2b) – the top of this hill should be much lower than Mount Fuji. Add two of the blue hill strips overlapping each other (Figs 2c and 2d), followed by a striped strip to represent a forest (Fig 2e), decreasing the angle of the strips as you go so that the stripes in the forest are vertical. Add the remaining blue hill strip (Fig 2f), then the final striped fabric for the rushes (Fig 2g). Pin the strips in place and stitch several vertical rows of running stitch in dark blue (Fig 2h); I stitched all the way to the top of the backing fabric on my picture, but just to the top of the strips will be enough.

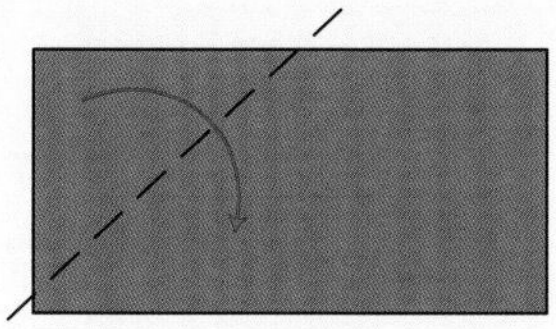

Fig 1a

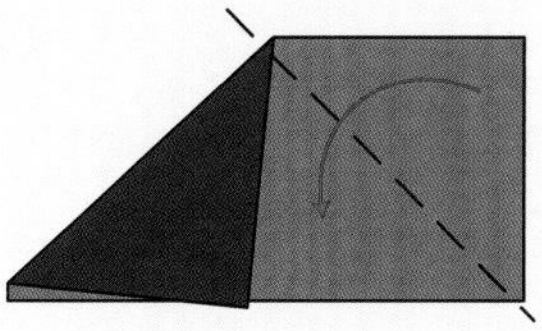

Fig 1b

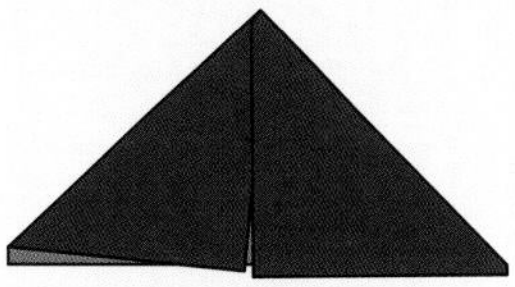

Fig 1c

Fig 2a

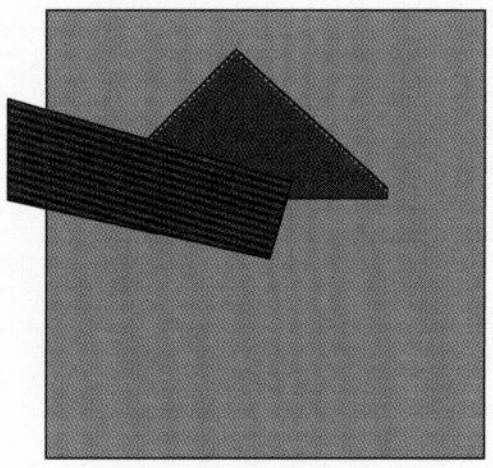

Fig 2b

Fig 2c

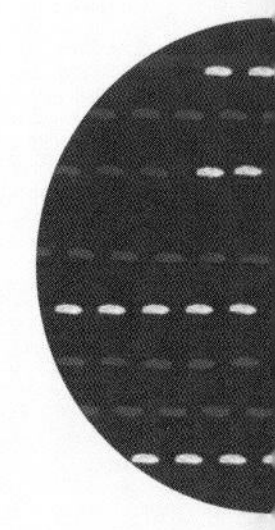

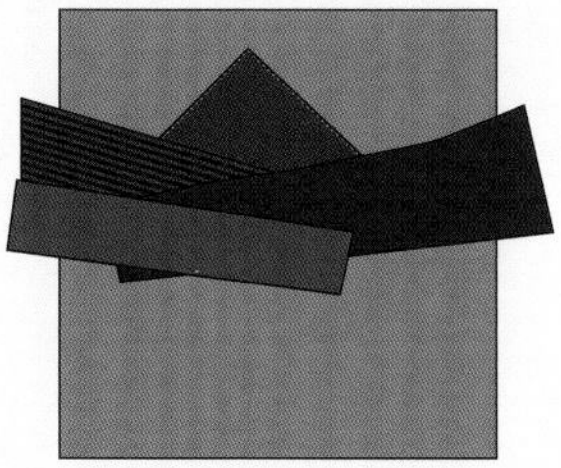

Fig 2d

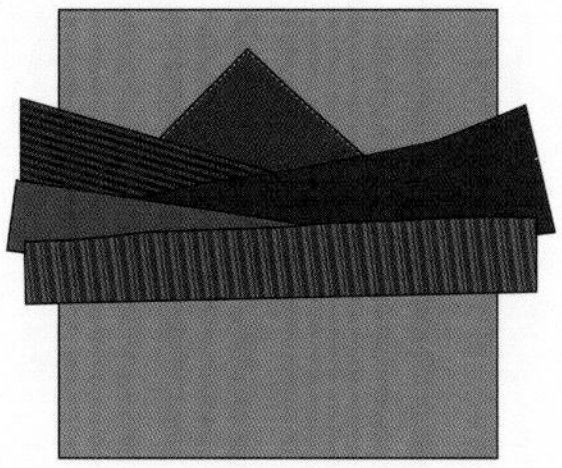

Fig 2e

Fig 2f

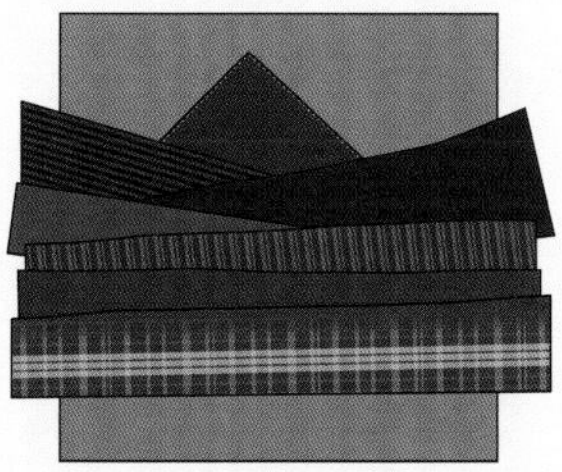

Fig 2g

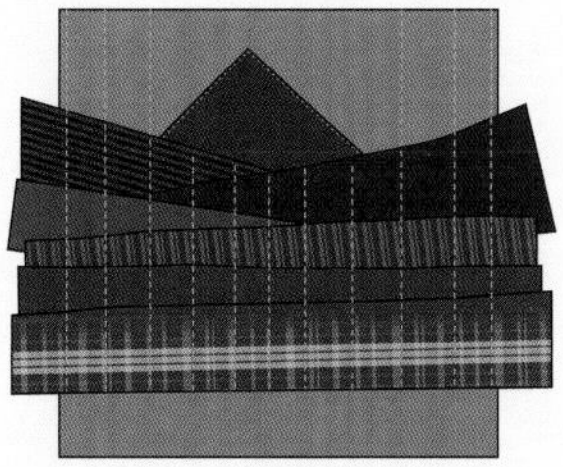

Fig 2h

3 Add stitched details: Using white sashiko thread to represent snow, sew a running stitch line approx. ⅛in (3mm) from the raw edge along the top of each of the hills. On Mount Fuji, stitch the lines of snow radiating out from the summit. Use blue-and-white variegated sashiko thread to stitch vertical lines to represent the forest. Use cream sashiko thread to stitch vertical lines of varying heights close together for the lakeside rushes.

4 Now stitch the moonlit sky. First, mark the moon circle in the area to the left of Mount Fuji, using a white fabric marker or a pencil to draw around the base of a cotton reel or similar round object with a diameter of approx. 1½in (3.8cm). Starting at the outside of the circle, use white sashiko thread to stitch in a closely worked spiral so that the moon appears quite solid. Using the variegated sashiko thread, stitch horizontal lines across the foundation fabric for the impression of thin clouds.

5 Add the lake fabric: Turn under ¼in (6mm) along one long edge of the light blue fabric strip. Making sure that it is perfectly horizontal across the picture, pin the folded edge of the lake strip over the rushes strip and appliqué stitch it in place using dark blue sashiko thread. Using the variegated sashiko thread, stitch horizontal lines across the lake to suggest water ripples. Use white sashiko thread to add a few extra rows of stitches to suggest the moon's reflection.

6 Frame the picture: Take the picture frame's backing board and, working on the front side, apply lines of double-sided adhesive tape close to the edge. Stick the picture to the backing board, checking that it is straight and smooth. Trim the edges of the fabric, then fasten the board into the frame.

greetings card miniature

This miniature version of the Mount Fuji landscape requires even smaller amounts of fabrics and threads and utilizes an old shirt button for the moon. Cut the foundation fabric approx. ½in (1.3cm) larger than the aperture on a tri-fold card. I used fabric selvedges to suggest the lakeside forests and a striped fabric for the lake, and I stitched the starry sky with tiny random cross stitches. Use double-sided adhesive tape to adhere the finished piece to the card aperture.

messenger bag

Most of us have an old pair of jeans we love but that are just a bit too tight to wear anymore, so why not recycle them to make this useful bag? Beneath the bag flap you'll find that the top half of the messenger bag is made from the waistband and hip area of a pair of denims, cut off just below the back pockets, providing lots of handy compartments for your stuff! But the repurposing doesn't end there – the ripped knee fabric was included in the boro-patched base panel, the strap was made from one of the legs, and the top fly button became the fastener for the bag flap. The bag base has boxed-out corners to make it nice and roomy, and the zip fly can be unfastened to get larger items in or out of the slightly tapered bag top. The seed-stitch detailing used for the boro gives this piece a more contemporary style.

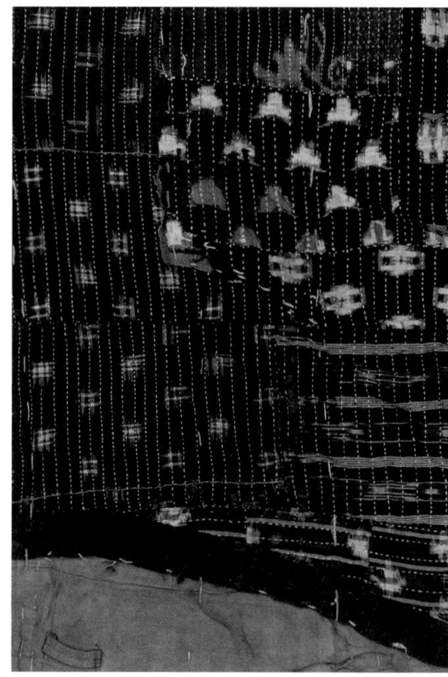

my inspiration

An old pair of cotton trousers (pants) peeks out of the corner of this small but very thick bodoko *(boro cloth), thought to have been used as a child's futon. Without dismantling it, there is no way of knowing just what else is inside. The rest of the boro repurposes several neatly pieced and closely sashiko-stitched* noragi *work jackets, made from a wide selection of beautiful* kasuri *(ikat), striped and stencilled fabrics – a true collection of textile treasures.*

you will need

- One pair of jeans, size 28–32in (71–81cm) waist, for the bag top panel and straps*
- One piece of plain cotton fabric 14 x 23in (35.6 x 58.4cm), for the bag base panel**
- Two pieces of plain cotton fabric 14 x 15in (35.6 x 38.1cm), for the bag flap (outer and lining)**
- Assorted fabric scraps recycled or new, including plains, prints and weaves, 2in (5cm) square and larger squares/strips, for the patches
- 50in (127cm) approx. 1¼in (3.2cm) wide bias strips, for trimming the bag strap
- 109yd (100m) fine or medium sashiko thread in blue, dark red and blue-and-white variegated
- Buttonhole thread (optional)
- Machine sewing thread to tone with fabrics
- Circle template, 5in (12.7cm) diameter or similar
- Basic sewing kit (see Tools and Materials)

Jeans larger than 32in (81cm) will make more of a holdall-sized bag.

***The size of your jeans will determine the size of the bag base panel and the bag flap, so you may need to make adjustments to these fabric measurements – see steps 1 and 2 for more guidance.*

1 Make the bag top: Mark out the cutting lines on the hip section of your jeans. On the front, there needs to be about 1in (2.5cm) of fabric left below the fly opening, and on the back, a similar amount underneath the bottom edge of the back pockets so that the bag base panel can be attached. To accommodate this, I needed to cut my jeans on a slight curve rather than cutting them straight. To ensure that your markings are symmetrical, start by drawing your cutting line across one half of the front of the jeans (from the fly opening to the side edge), then mirror the curve on the other side (Fig 1). Repeat to mark the cutting line on the back of the jeans (Fig 2). Ideally, the cutting lines front and back should meet at the fold at the sides of the jeans when they are laid flat (it is worth noting from the diagrams that this usually doesn't line up with the side seams of the jeans). It doesn't matter if the front is slightly higher or lower than the back, but it will make bag asssembly easier in step 7 if they are fairly even.

2 The front pocket bags may extend below your marked cutting lines, so pin them up out of the way before cutting out the top panel shape. Retain the rest of the jeans, as you will need one of the legs to make the bag strap in step 15 and other areas of the denim can be used for the boro patching. There is no need to finish the cut edges, as these will be covered with patches when the bag is finished.

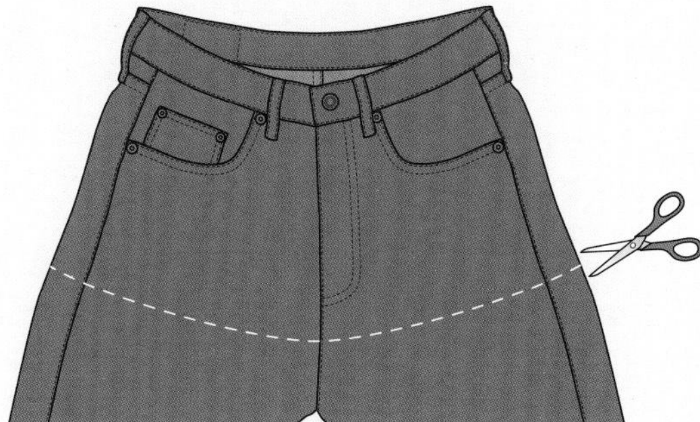

Fig 1

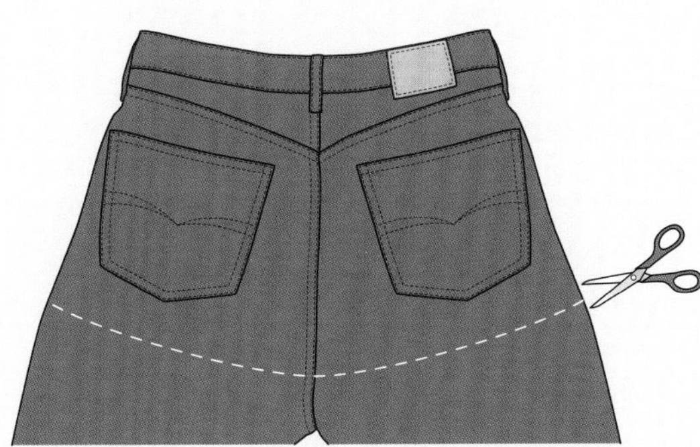

Fig 2

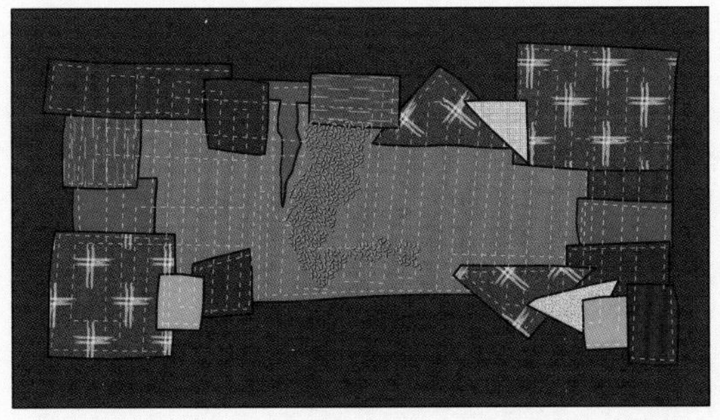

Fig 3

3 Determine the size of the base panel: Measure a straight line across the widest point of the bag top shape. On my jeans, this measured 21½in (54.6cm). I added on an extra ¾in (2cm) at each side for the seam allowances*, to cut my bag base panel at 14 x 23in (35.6 x 58.4cm). I used a traditional narrow-width Japanese fabric for my bag base panel, as this was the perfect size when turned on its side.

**The finished seam allowance is likely to be ½in (1.3cm) but adding on ¾in (2cm) at this stage allows for the panel pulling in a little with all the dense stitching and patching.*

4 Add fabric patches to the base panel: Begin the boro patching on the base panel using a variety of fabrics, including some of the remaining denim fabric from the jeans, following the advice in Techniques: Patchwork for Boro and referring to Fig 3. I used the ripped part of one of the knees across the centre of the panel, which will become the bag base in step 5. Continue to add a mixture of patches – some with turned edges, some with raw edges, some cut on the bias or with bias edges, as this will help to vary the amount of fraying when the bag is in use – hand sewing each patch in place with running stitch. At each end of the panel, leave approx. 2in (5cm) unpatched (these patches will be added later). Do remember to take into account the boxed-out corners that will be made once the bag is constructed in steps 5 and 6; don't add too many layers there just yet, and avoid using denim in this area so that the panel doesn't become too bulky. Add some dense seed stitch to various areas of the patching, stitching at random.

5 Construct the bag base: Fold the panel in half so that the long ends meet, with the boro-patching on the outside of the bag base, and pin the side seams in place. The seams will be on the outside, but hidden with more patches. Before sewing up the side seams, check the width of the patched panel against the straight-line measurement taken across the top panel in step 2, then sew up the side seam either by machine or by hand (with backstitch, or two rows of running stitch worked one on top of the other) using at least a ½in (1.3cm) seam allowance, taking a slightly larger or smaller seam allowance as required to ensure that the base panel will fit the jeans bag top when joined in step 7. Press the seam allowance to one side and use a handsewn running stitch to stitch it down. Add some more patches on the outside of the bag, covering the top of the seam area. Machine or hand sew the side seam on the other side of the base panel, then add some extra patches as before (Fig 4).

6 With the bag base turned right side out, box-out the corners, stitching 1½in (3.8cm) away from the corner point (see Techniques: Making Up Projects). Do not trim the corner points but fold them up the sides of the bag base and stitch them in place using appliqué hem stitch. Cover the corner points with more patches, which can extend under the bag as well. Add plenty of running stitch in this area, to strengthen the corners. Fold over the top of the bag base to the right side by ½in (1.3cm) all around, and tack (baste) in place.

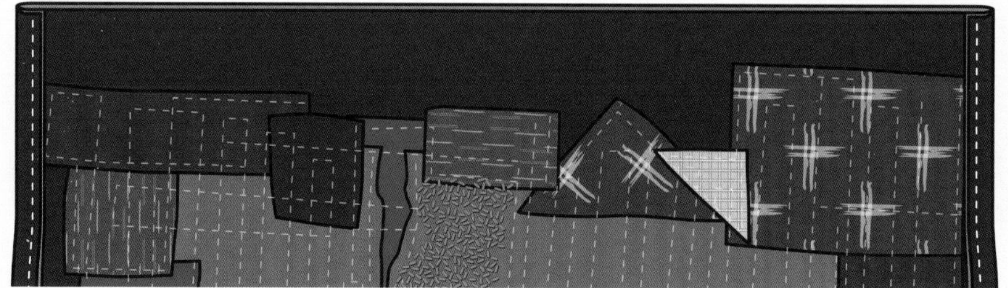

Fig 4

7 Sew the bag base to the bag top: Lay the jeans bag top flat and mark the side points top with pins. Line up and pin the side seams of the bag base to these points, so that the jeans bag top lies flat over the top of the bag base (Fig 5). The patched bag base goes up inside the jeans hip section at the top of the bag; note that the top of the patched bag base does not follow the curved edge of the jeans, but goes straight across, as indicated by the dashed red line in the diagram. The denim layers will overlap the bag base by ½in (1.3cm) at the sides, but by a lot more towards the centre of the front and back. Note that the edges of the denim layers are left raw and not turned under (these will be covered with patches in step 8). Keeping the front pocket bags of the jeans pinned up out of the way, ease the bag base to the bag top, and pin all around the shaped edge of the bag top to secure it to the bag base. Hand sew running stitch about ¼in (6mm) from the raw edge of the denim all the way around, stitching through to the bag base layer beneath as shown as shown by the dashed blue line in Fig 5.

8 Turn the bag inside out and hem the folded top edge of the bag base to the denim all the way around. Turn the bag back through to the right side. Add additional boro fabric patches to cover the raw edges of the denim.

9 Prepare the bag flap panels: I have given an approximate measurement for the two pieces of fabric (outer and lining) required for the bag flap, but this may need to be altered depending on the size of your jeans, so check your measurements before cutting out your fabrics. Allowing 2in (5cm) on each side of the top (waistband) of the jeans bag top for attaching the bag straps, measure the space between to give you the finished width of your bag flap. Now measure from the top of the jeans waistband to the bottom of the bag base to give you the finished height of your bag flap. Add 1in (2.6cm) to each measurement for the seam allowances, and this gives you the size required for each bag flap fabric panel.

10 Mark the curves at the bottom corners of both the bag flap outer and lining panels, using the 5in (12.7cm) circle template or something similarly sized (Fig 6).

Fig 5

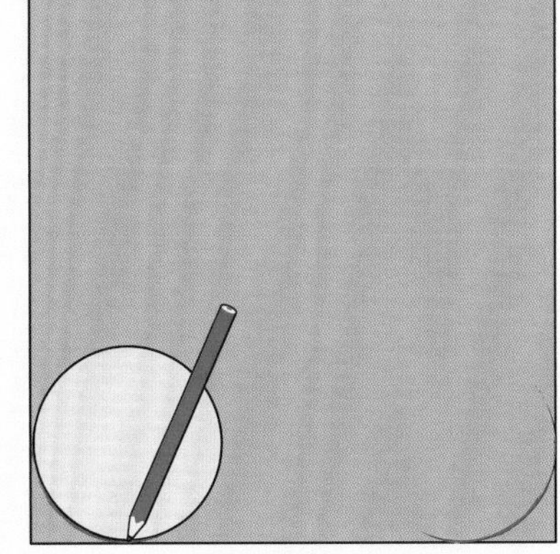

Fig 6

11 Add patches to the bag flap outer panel: Use running stitch and sashiko thread to hand sew patches to the bag flap outer panel, avoiding the area outside the bottom corner curves as these will be trimmed off later. Think about where the flap will get the most wear – across the top, at the bottom edge and around the buttonhole area (see step 19 for a rough idea of the buttonhole position) – and add more patches there. Use a mixture of patches just as you did for the base panel in step 4, and do add extra lines of running stitch.

12 Make the bag flap: Trim the bottom corner curves on both the patched outer panel and the lining panel. Place the trimmed panels right sides together (Fig 7), pinning the lining (grey) to the patched panel (dark blue), setting the edge of the lining back by ⅛in (3mm) on the side and bottom edges to create a *susofuki* (hem wipe); this will protect the edge of the bag flap with the lining while adding a decorative detail. The lining will seem a little baggy as you do this. Pin the sides first, then centre and pin across the bottom edge, before easing the curved corners into position.

13 Sew the bag flap layers together either by machine or by handsewn backstitch with a ½in (⅓cm) seam allowance (measured from the edge of the patched panel not the lining), leaving the top edge unsewn. Clip at the curves to within ⅛in (3mm) of the stitching, then turn the bag flap through to the right side.

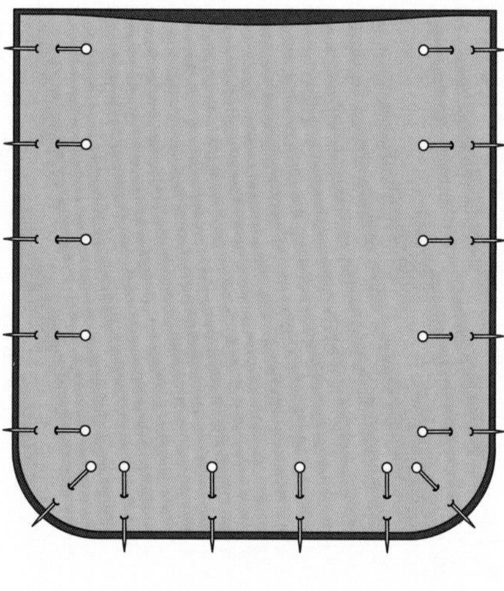

Fig 7

14 Press the stitched edges, allowing a scant 1⁄16in (1–2mm) of the lining to roll to the front, and pin. Hand sew from the lining side using the *mimi-guke* edge stitch (see Techniques: Traditional Boro Stitches), stitching through the lining and seam allowances only (do not sew through to the outside) to hold the *susofuki* in place, leaving 1in (2.5cm) unsewn at the top edges. Turn the raw edges of the top edge of the bag flap inwards by 1in (2.5cm) and hand sew using ladder stitch.

15 **Make the bag strap:** Use one of the retained jeans legs to make your bag strap. First decide how long you want your bag strap to be. If you intend to carry the bag across your body, the strap will need to be longer. Cut the strap a little longer than you need, then pin it to the bag temporarily to determine the correct length for you. I made the finished length of my strap 56in (142cm), and added an extra 2in (5cm) to each end to stitch it to the bag sides. This required a much longer length than the jeans leg, so I machine stitched two 4in (10.2in) wide strips together with a diagonal seam cut on a 45-degree angle (Fig 8), pressing the seam open to avoid a bulky join. Trim off the 'dog ears' or points on either side.

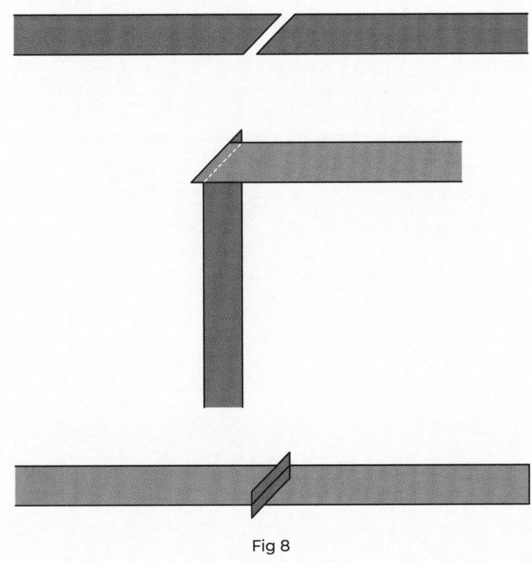

Fig 8

16 Fold the bag strap strip in half along its length and open out. Then press each edge to the centre fold line (Fig 9a). Use sashiko thread to hand sew a line of running stitch about ¼in (6mm) from the edge along each side of the strap. The denim will be quite tough to stitch through, so use a thimble and stab stitch if necessary. Using the 1¼in (3.2cm) wide bias strips, cover the raw edges of the denim along the centre of the bag strap, hand sewing running stitch about ¼in (6mm) from each edge of the bias strip, overlapping one strip with the next by about 1in (2.5cm) as required (Fig 9b). Add an extra line of running stitch down the centre of the bias strip. The strip edges will fray attractively when the finished bag is washed.

17 Sew bag flap to top of bag: The bag flap is handsewn just inside the back top edge of the bag using two rows of ladder stitch and avoiding stitching through the jeans belt loops. Pin the centre top of the flap to the inside top edge of the jeans waistband, overlapping the flap by about 1in (2.5cm), and pin all the way along the join. Stitch one row of ladder stitch, working from the inside, along the edge of the bag flap. Sew the second row of ladder stitch from the outside, just below the topstitching on the jeans waistband. Start and finish with a few stitches in the opposite direction, as well as a knot buried between the layers.

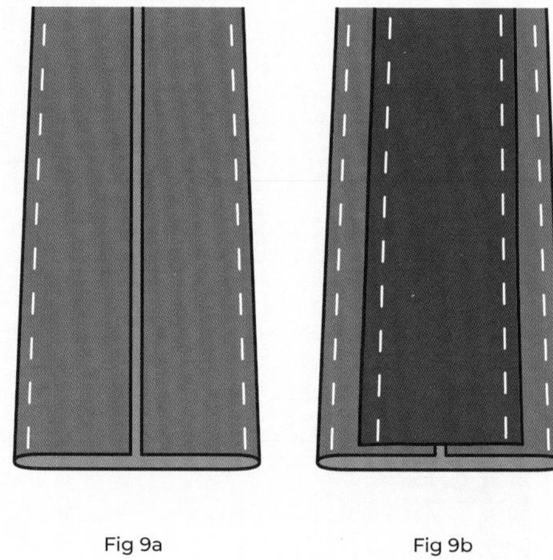

Fig 9a Fig 9b

18 Sew bag strap to either side of bag flap: If your calculations have been correct, the strap ends will fit to either side of the flap, but don't worry if they are not quite perfect. Overlap each end of the strap on the inside of the bag by 3in (7.6cm) approx., without folding the ends under. First pin, then hand sew one end in place using sashiko thread and running stitch worked in an X formation. Once one end of the strap has been sewn, pin the other end in place and try the bag on, to check you are happy with the length, then stitch as before. Cut a patch about 3 x 2in (7.6 x 5cm) to cover each end of the strap, and fold under by ¼in (6mm) all round; pin, then stitch in place.

19 Sewing the buttonhole: The bag flap fastens using the jeans fly button. Fill the bag with something to pad it out slightly so that you can work out where the buttonhole needs to be when the bag is in use. You will be able to feel the position of the button slightly through the bag flap. Mark this point with a pin. Draw a vertical line to mark the buttonhole slit, which needs to be slightly longer than the button itself, marking a circle with a scant ¼in (5mm) diameter at the end of the line (when the bag is fastened, the button shank will sit in the circle area). Using a very short stitch length, machine sew about ¹⁄₁₆in (2mm) on either side of your marked line, including around the circle. Snip the fabric between your stitched lines and check that this is large enough for the button to go through (it needs to be slightly loose at this stage). Once you are happy with the fit, refer to Fig 10 to buttonhole stitch around the cut-out shape, using either sashiko or buttonhole thread.

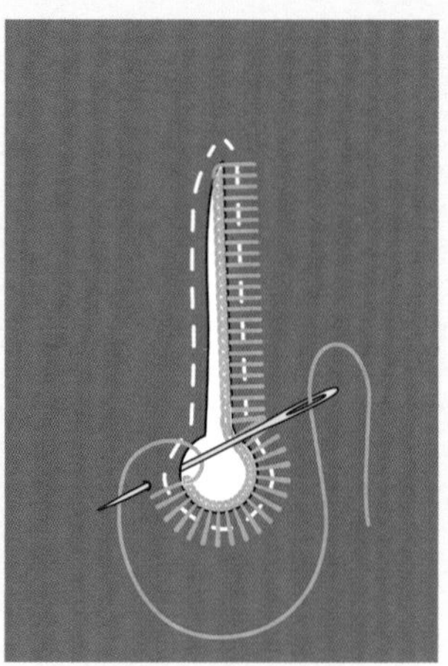

Fig 10

20 Machine wash the finished bag at 40–60 °C, which will slightly wrinkle the boro and help both to 'set' the stitches and to fluff up the raw edges on the patches. This will give a very attractive frayed edge finish to the bias strap. Press the bag flap to restore its shape.

gadget slipcase

You could use the remaining jeans leg to make a gadget slipcase, with a little extra boro added across the bottom half. First, measure your gadget and cut a section from the jeans leg that is wider and longer than your item – I liked the look of the ripped knee area. Check the panel for size by wrapping it around your gadget – it needs to be around ½in (⅓cm) larger all around. Unpick one of the side seams, leaving the topstitched seam in place. Hand sew some extra fabric patches to cover the back of any ripped areas, then add a few extra patches here and there across the bottom of the panel. Sew the base and side seams following steps 10 and 11 of the tote bag project but omitting the boxed-out corners. Bind the top edge with 1¼in (3.2cm) bias strip, folded under on the inside but leaving a raw edge on the outside.

hanten jacket

The *hanten* (half wear) jacket is traditional Japanese work wear. Many were boro, pieced from various large scraps, with extra patches added as they became worn. I used new fabrics, including stripes, plaids and wovens, pieced in a simple machine-sewn strip patchwork for both the outer and lining of my hanten, hand stitching the piecing seam allowances down with a cream sashiko running stitch before making up the jacket. The sleeves are tapered and a straight collar, complete with collar cover, runs from one hem to the other, making it easy to wear either loose or with a narrow obi sash. Raw-edge vintage and recycled fabric patches are hand stitched to areas that are likely to become worn quickly, such as the shoulders and the cuffs. Just like a favourite pair of jeans, this jacket will become more beautiful as it is worn. One size fits most, but to make it larger or smaller, simply alter the length and width of the panels slightly.

my inspiration

This antique donza, a kind of work jacket dating from the late-nineteenth century, has a stunning selection of late Edo-era kasuri *(ikat) cotton fabrics, with subtle, small designs. The upper part of the pieced lining is natural hemp. It has two sets of stitches holding the layers together, added at different times. Wear and tear and patched repairs all add to the jacket's wonderful patina and true boro feeling.*

you will need

- Two pieces of patchwork 84 x 15in (213.4 x 38.1cm), for the body outer*
- Two pieces of patchwork 23 x 16½in (58.4 x 41.9cm), for the sleeve outer*
- Two pieces of patchwork 84 x 15in (213.4 x 38.1cm), for the body lining*
- Two pieces of patchwork 23 x 16½in (58.4 x 41.9cm), for the sleeve lining*
- One piece of plain dark blue cotton 100 x 6½in (254 x 16.5cm), for the collar**
- One piece of fabric 7 x 6½in (17.8 x 16.5cm), for the collar reinforcement
- One piece of plain dark blue cotton approx. 30 x 6½in (76.2 x 16.5cm), for the collar cover
- Assorted scraps of recycled fabric in various sizes, for the patches
- 110yd (100m) fine sashiko thread in cream
- Oddments of dark blue and black sashiko thread to match patches
- Machine sewing thread
- Basic sewing kit (see Tools and Materials)

**For further advice on the patchwork piecing, including fabric quantities, see step 1.*

*** The collar can be pieced from two 51in (129.5cm) strips if you prefer.*

1 Tips for piecing the body and sleeve panels: To make the hanten body and sleeve panels, I have machine sewn new fabrics in a simple strip patchwork, using darker colours for the outer (Fig 1a) and lighter colours for the lining (Fig 1b). To create the cuff, a 2¼ x 23in (5.7 x 58.4cm) strip of fabric was added to the wrist end of each sleeve. The exact amount of fabric required will depend on how many patchwork seams are sewn, but as a rough guide your fabric pieces will need to amount to approx. 2⅛yd (2m) of 42– 43in (107–109cm) wide fabric for the outer and the same again for the lining. Machine sew the patchwork strips with a ⅜in (1cm) seam allowance. Press the seams to one side; then, working from the right side and approx. ⅛in (3mm) from the seam, hand sew running stitch with cream sashiko thread for a topstitch effect. Patchwork-style cheater fabrics can be used to give the illusion of more elaborate piecing, but do add cream 'topstitching' along any faux seams so they look real.

Seams are ⅜in (1cm) throughout, unless stated otherwise. Start and finish all machine-sewn garment construction seams with a few reverse stitches.

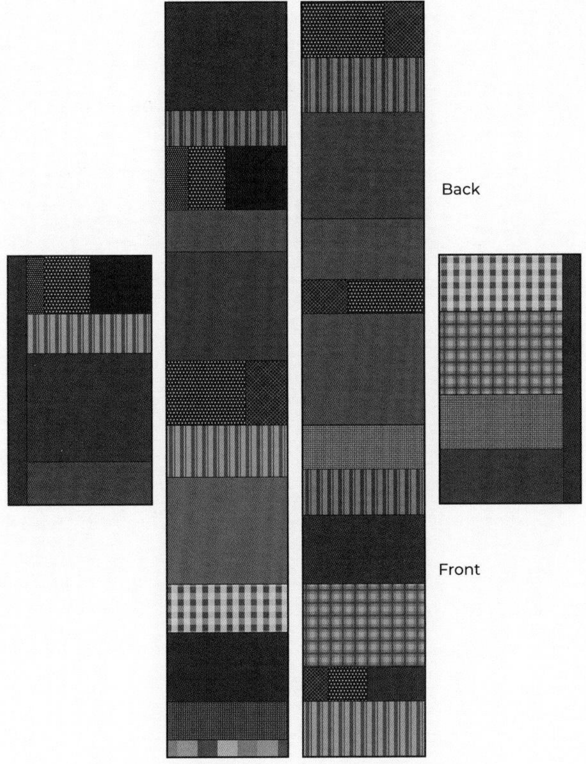

Fig 1a: Piecing for hanten outer

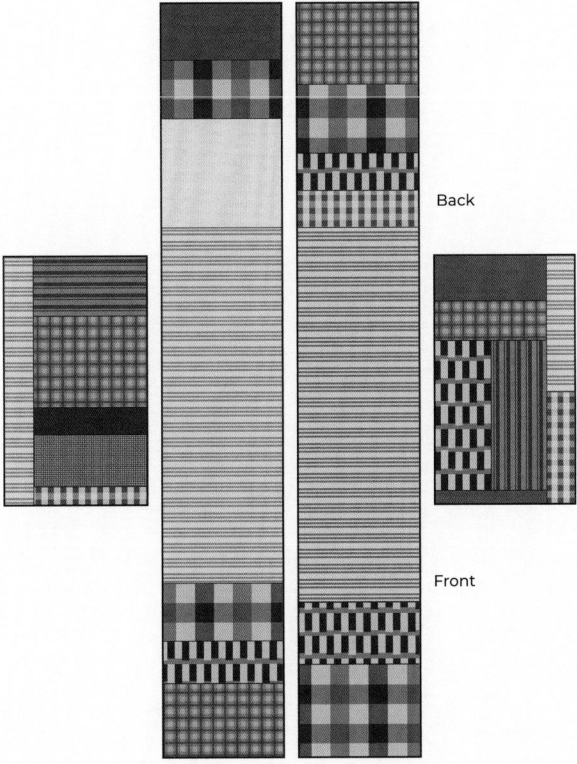

Fig 1b: Piecing for hanten lining

2 Cut the collar neck shaping in the body outer and lining panels: Make a copy of the neck shaping template (Fig 2). Fold each body outer panel in half so that the short ends meet, wrong sides facing, with the back of each panel facing you. Draw around the neck shaping template along the folded edge (the shoulder line) of each body outer panel, as shown in Fig 3. Remember, you are making a right and a left body panel, so one will mirror the other. Cut along the drawn line through the *back* of the body panel only (Fig 4). Repeat to cut the collar neck shaping on the lining panels.

3 Machine sew the centre back seam: Line up the two body outer panels, right sides together, pin along the centre back seam and machine stitch. Press the seam to the left, using the *kise* fold if you wish (see Techniques: Making Up Projects). Repeat to sew the centre back seam of the body lining panels but this time press the seam to the right; it needs to lie in the same direction as the hanten jacket body when the body and lining are sewn together, as explained in step 11.

4 Make the sleeves: Referring to Fig 5, take one of the sleeve outer panels and fold it in half, right sides together, with the fold running along the top of the sleeve. Measure 9in (23cm) down at the wrist end and mark with a cross ⅜in (1cm) from the edge (A). Now mark a cross ⅜in (1cm) from the opposite lower corner (B) and draw a line between the crosses. Pin, then machine sew along the drawn line to make the sleeve seam, starting and finishing at the cross marks. Repeat for the remaining sleeve outer panel and each of the sleeve lining panels. Trim the seam allowances to ⅜in (1cm) to reduce bulk and press open. Hold the seam allowances open on each sleeve (outers and linings) with two rows of cream running stitch.

5 Machine sew the side seams: With right sides together, pin the side seams on the body outer, leaving an opening of 11⅛in (28.3cm) from the top of the shoulder fold for the sleeves. Check the sleeve openings against the sleeve for length and adjust if necessary. Machine sew the side seams and press towards the front (Fig 6). Repeat for the body lining (you can use the *kise* fold on the seam if you choose to).

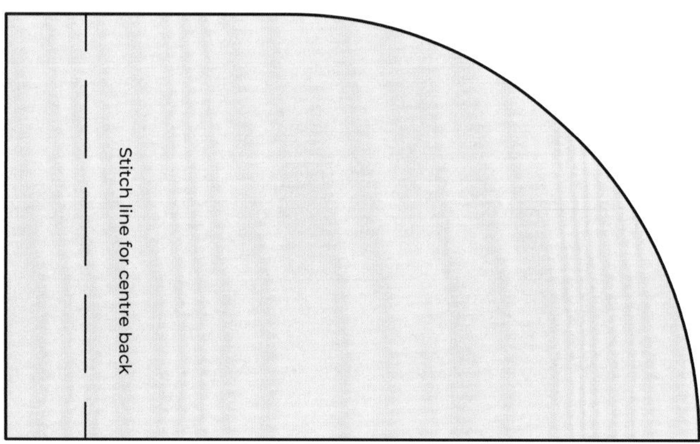

Fig 2: Neck shaping template

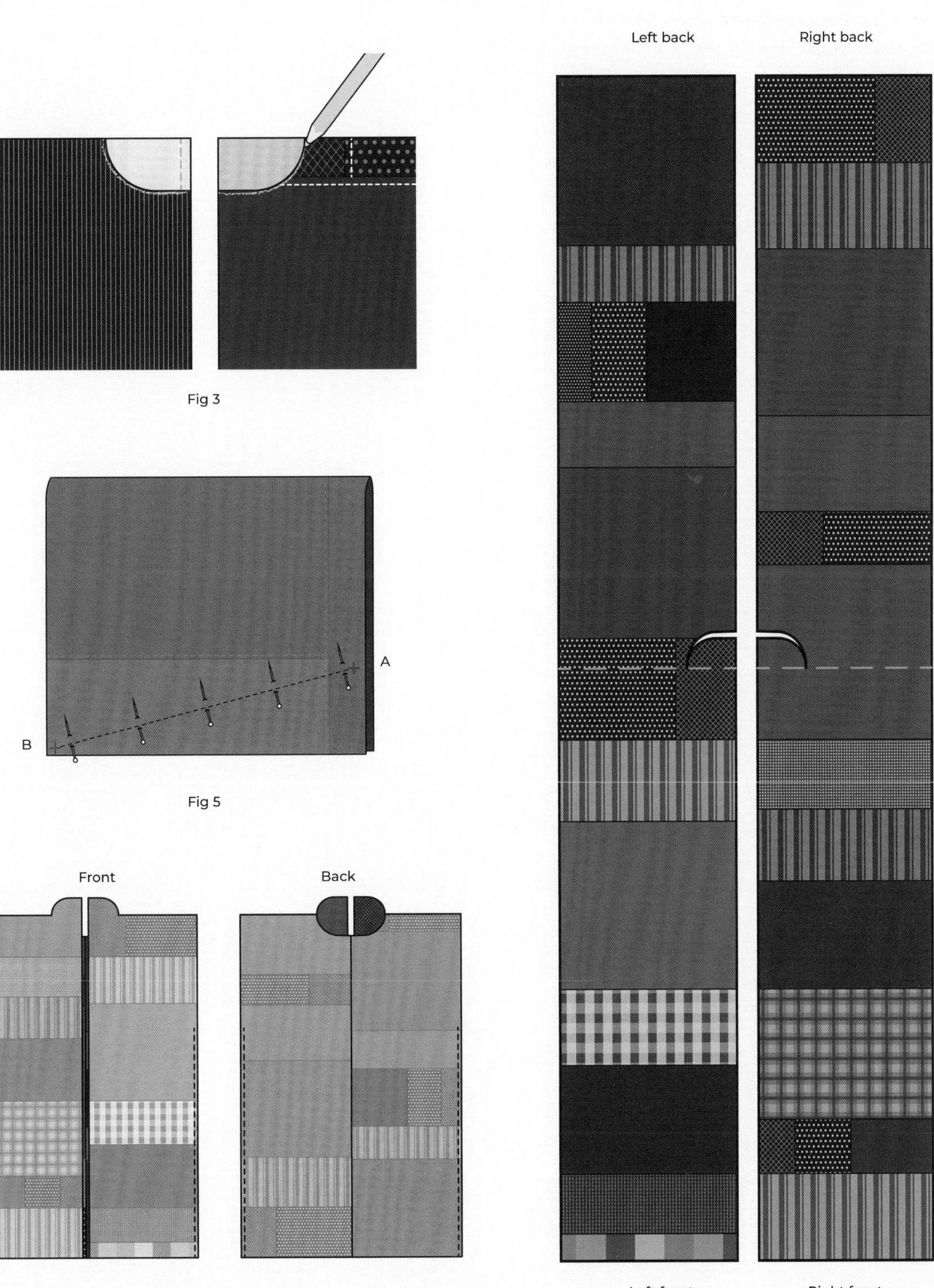

Fig 3

Fig 5

Fig 6

Fig 4

6 Insert the sleeves: With the body wrong side out and the sleeve right side out, i.e. with the the body and sleeve right side together, pin a sleeve outer into the sleeve opening of the body outer, making sure the seam on the underside of the sleeve matches up with the body side seam around the sleeve opening. Machine sew the sleeve to the body (Fig 7). Repeat to sew the second sleeve into the other sleeve opening. Press the seam allowances towards the body and hold in place with a row of cream running stitch, from the right side. Repeat to sew each sleeve lining into the body lining (you can use the *kise* fold on the seam if you choose to).

7 Join the lining to the outer: Up to this point, we have been working on constructing the outer and the lining independently of each other. It is now time to join the lining to the outer, which we shall now refer to as the hanten. Start by joining at the right sleeve wrist opening. Turn the hanten right side out and the lining wrong side out. Slip the hanten into the lining, with the right sleeve inside the right lining sleeve, so that the right sides of the fabrics are facing each other. Pin the wrist edge of the sleeve to the wrist edge of the lining, making sure that the underarm seams are lined up, then machine sew around the wrist edge (Fig 8). Place your hand inside the right hanten sleeve and carefully pull all the lining fabric back through the sleeve and into the hanten. Now the lining is *inside* the hanten. Push the left sleeve lining down inside the left hanten sleeve, until the wrist opening is reached (Fig 9).

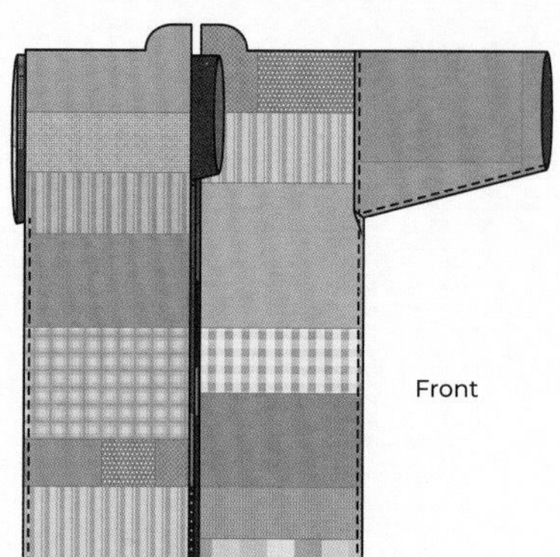

Fig 7

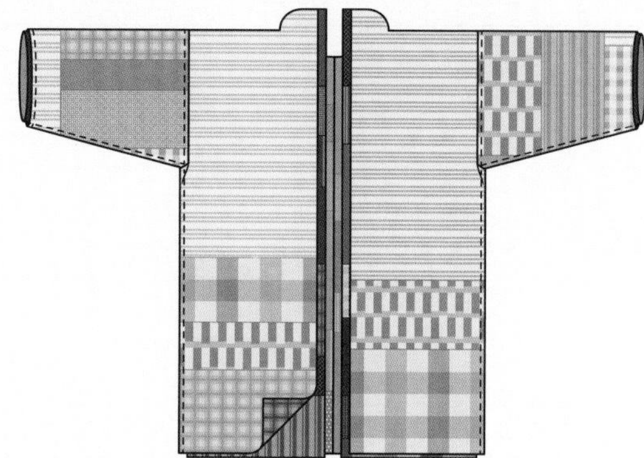
Fig 8

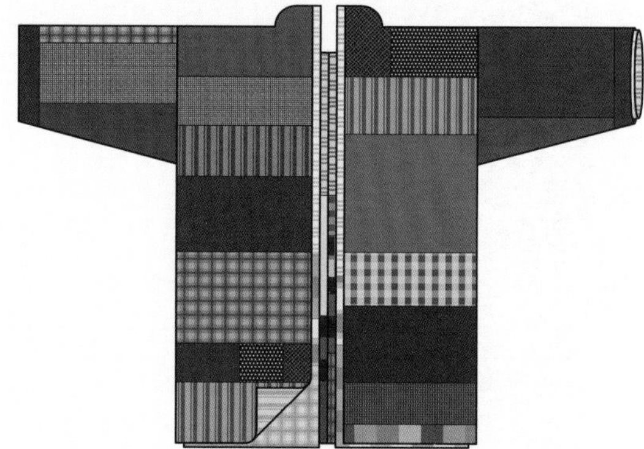
Fig 9

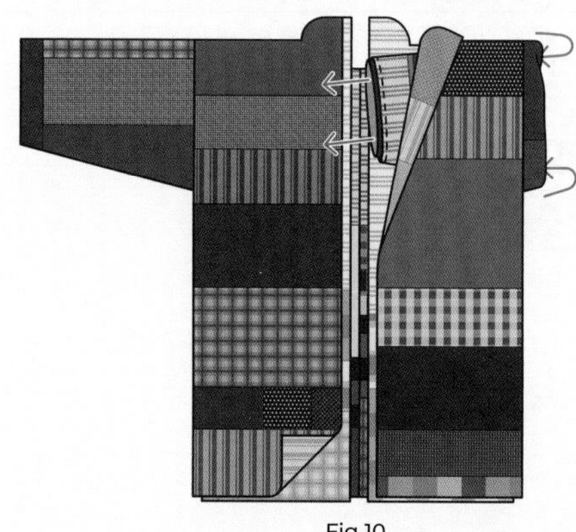
Fig 10

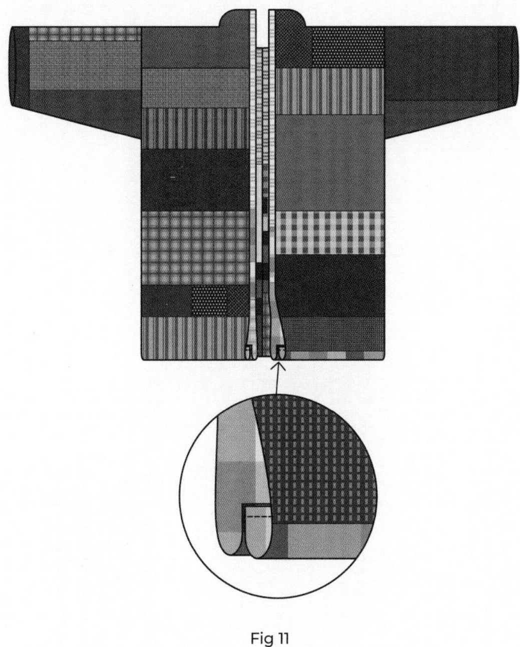

Fig 11

8 Now join the left sleeve lining to the left sleeve wrist opening. This is a tricky manoeuvre, and you will have to work in between the hanten and the lining, inside the sleeve. Place your hand between the lining and the hanten, going in through the top left of the chest and down the sleeve (Fig 10). Once again, make sure the underarm seams are lined up. Take hold of the wrist edges and, keeping them right sides together, pull the sleeve back out towards yourself, through the front of the hanten. As soon as you can, pin the lining to the hanten at the wrist, keeping right sides together and without letting go of the fabric. Continue to pin lining and hanten together around the wrist opening, then machine sew around the wrist, joining the lining to the hanten. The fabrics will seem very twisted as you sew, so work your way around the wrist opening slowly. If you find this very difficult, you can hand sew the lining to the sleeve around the wrist opening by simply turning back a ⅜in (1cm) hem on both hanten and lining and slip stitching them together.

9 Next, join the hanten and lining together along the lower edge. Once again, you will need to work with your hand in between the hanten and the lining to pin and machine sew the hem in place, making sure that the corresponding centre back and side seam allowances are lying directly on top of each other (Fig 11).

10 Finish the hem and sleeve openings: Press the hem and the sleeve openings, allowing a scant ⅛in (3mm) of the lining to roll to the front of these edges. This creates a *susofuki* (hem wipe), which protects the edge of the garment and looks pretty. Pin, then stitch in place from the lining side with the *mimi-guke* edge stitch (see Techniques: Traditional Boro Stitches), sewing through the lining and seam allowances only. This stitching should not be seen on the outside of the hanten. The photo shows the hem on the finished hanten.

11 Finish the body seams: Stitch the hanten body seam allowances to the lining seam allowances, first on the centre back seam, then on the side seams. This sewing detail, used for kimono, helps the garment to hang well, so that the outer and lining move as one without looking baggy. Slide your hand between the back of the hanten and the lining. If you have pressed the centre back seam allowances correctly, all four layers of fabric in the seam allowance will be lying in the same direction, to the left of the hanten. Starting at the back of the neck, pin the hanten seam allowance to the lining seam allowance, going as far down the back as you can reach (you won't be able to go right to the bottom hem, but close enough). Hand sew long running stitches through all layers a fraction of an inch (a couple of millimetres) from the centre back seam (Fig 12). Repeat for the side seams, this time working through the front gap between the hanten and the lining.

12 Prepare to attach the collar: The collar secures the outer and lining layers of the hanten along the front edges and around the back of the neck. First, tack (baste) the front edge of the hanten and the lining together. Draw a vertical line from the edge of the collar cut to the hem at either side (Fig 13). (The excess fabric at the front of the hanten is folded into the collar in lieu of any other reinforcement and is not trimmed away.) Now tack (baste) the layers together around the back of the neck, ½in (1.3cm) from the curved edge. Clip the curved edge slightly (Fig 14).

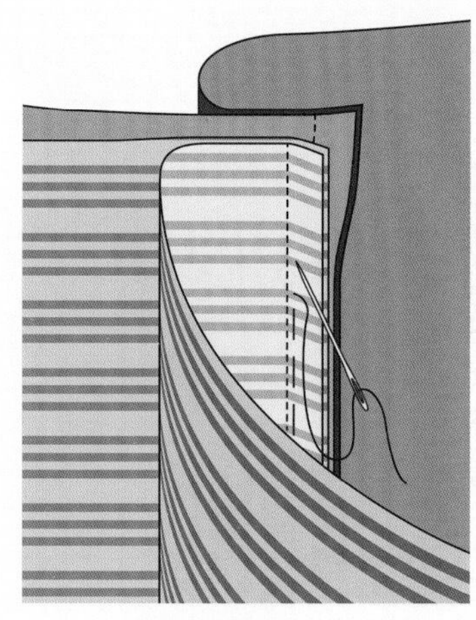

Fig 12

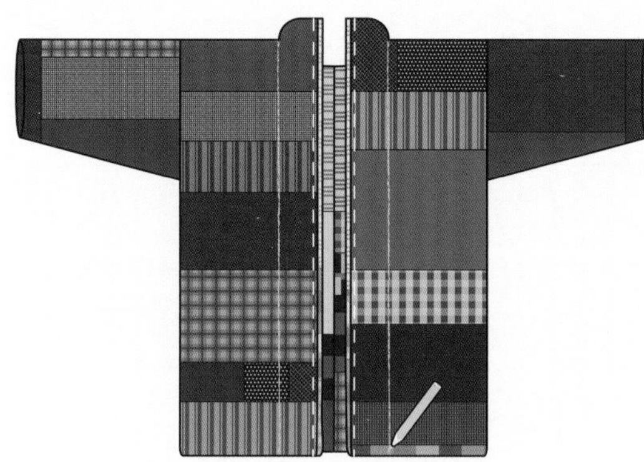

Fig 13

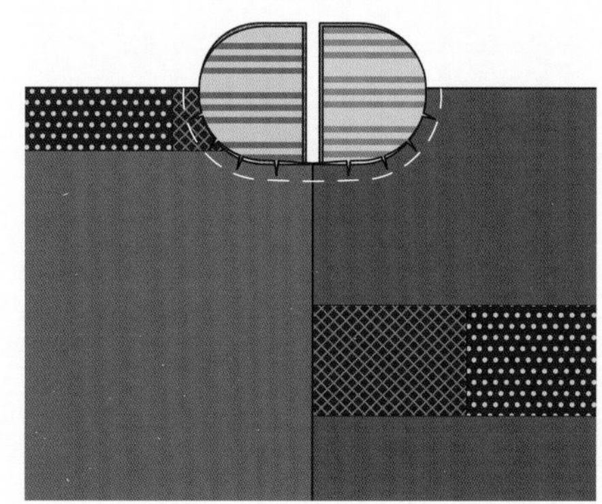

Fig 14

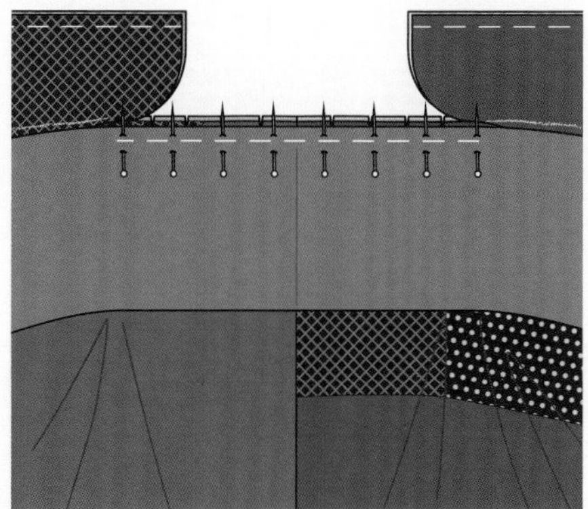

Fig 15

13 Attach the collar: Fold the 100 x 6½in (254 x 16.5cm) collar strip in half so that the short ends meet and crease to mark the centre. Line up the centre point of the collar strip with the centre back seam and the curve at the back of the neck, and pin to secure. Holding the curved collar cut as straight as possible, ease the collar strip to the back of the collar cut and pin in place as far as the top of the shoulder on both sides of the collar cut (Fig 15). Starting and finishing at the top of the shoulder, machine sew the collar to the neck of the hanten.

14 Machine stitch the collar to the neck and front edges: Line each end of the collar edge up with the vertical lines on either side of the front of the hanten, pin in place and machine sew. (Note that the collar strip is several inches/centimetres longer than the hem; this extra fabric will be folded and sewn into the ends of the collar in steps 16 and 17 to give it a little extra weight.) Sew the 7 x 6½in (17.8 x 16.5cm) collar reinforcement piece inside the collar at the back of the neck, as shown in Fig 16.

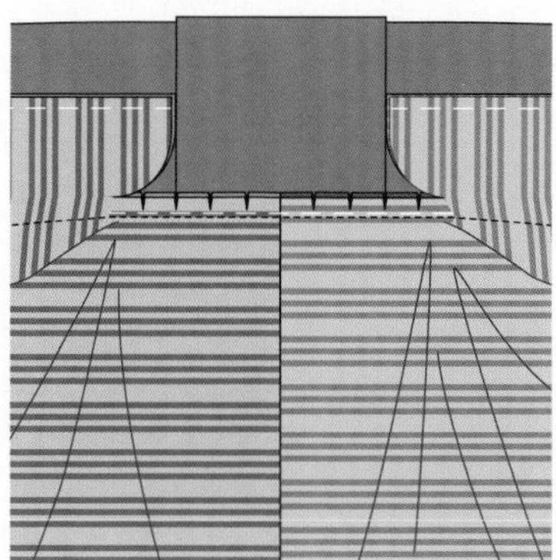

Fig 16

15 Prepare the collar strip for hand stitching: Press the collar strip over to the front edges of the hanten. Tack (baste) the edge of the hanten to the collar, as shown in Fig 17a, so that all three layers will move as one when the collar is folded in for hand stitching. Fold the unsewn edge of the collar strip back over the front edge of the hanten, and pin and tack (baste) as shown in Fig 17b. Notice how, at each end of the collar where it extends beyond the collar/body seam, the fabric has been slightly tapered in before pinning, so that it will tuck in as the collar is folded. Fold in the end of the collar strip at the hem and pin as shown in Fig 17c. Fold over the collar edge to line up with the machine-stitched line of the collar/body seam and pin (Fig 17d).

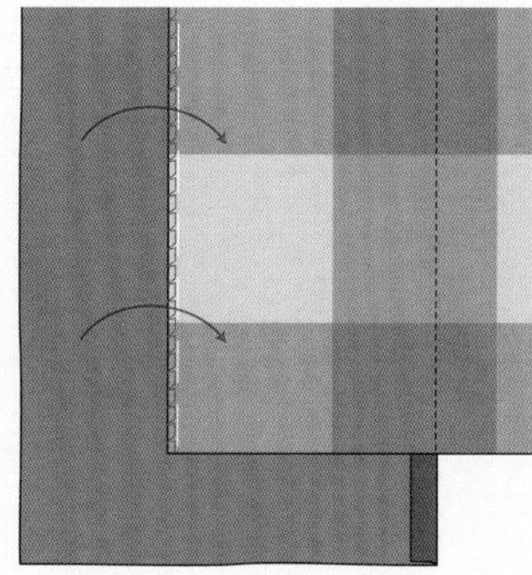

Fig 17a

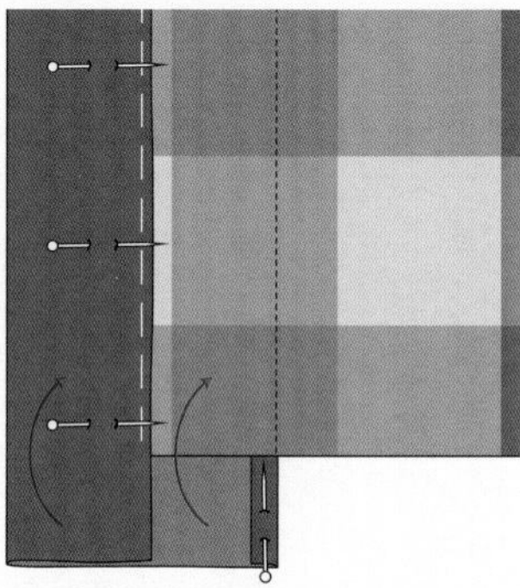

Fig 17b

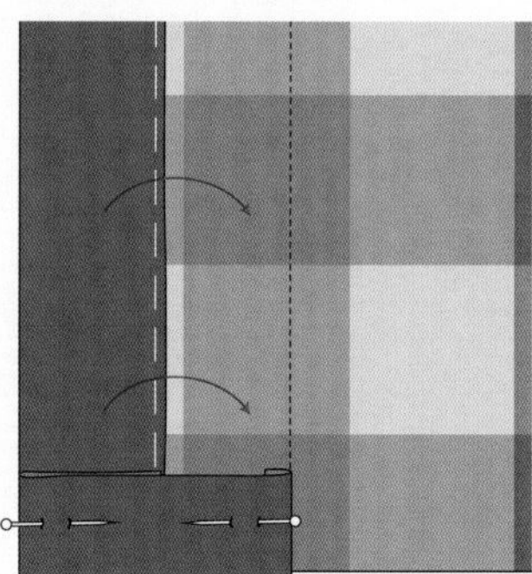

Fig 17c

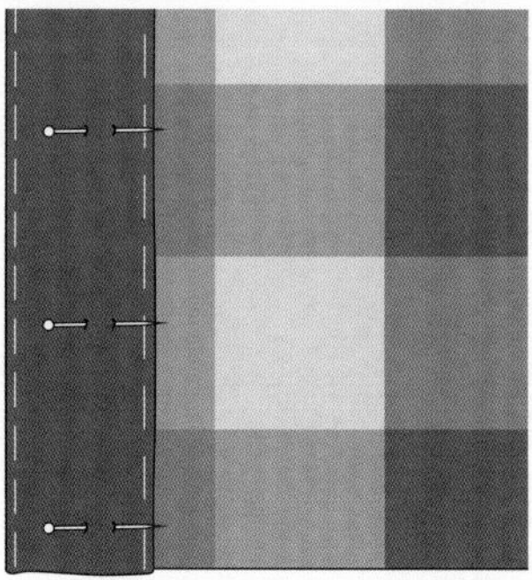

Fig 17d

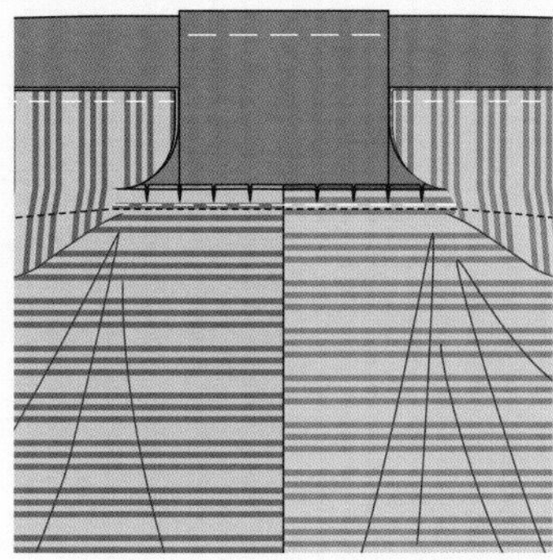
Fig 18

16 Just before folding over the back of the collar, tack (baste) one edge of the collar reinforcement inside the seam allowance between the collar and hanten body; then the other edge is tacked (basted) to the collar (make sure both the reinforcement and the collar are flat against each other at this stage) (Fig 18). Continue folding and pinning the collar ready for stitching. The other end of the collar is folded like a mirror image of Fig 17a–d.

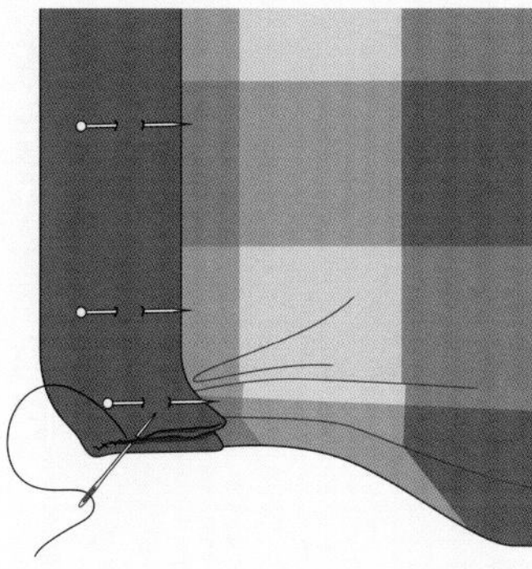
Fig 19

17 Hand stitch the folded edge of the collar in place: Start by slip stitching the ends of the collar at the hem at each side, as shown in Fig 19. Then continue to slip stitch the rest of the collar to the body.

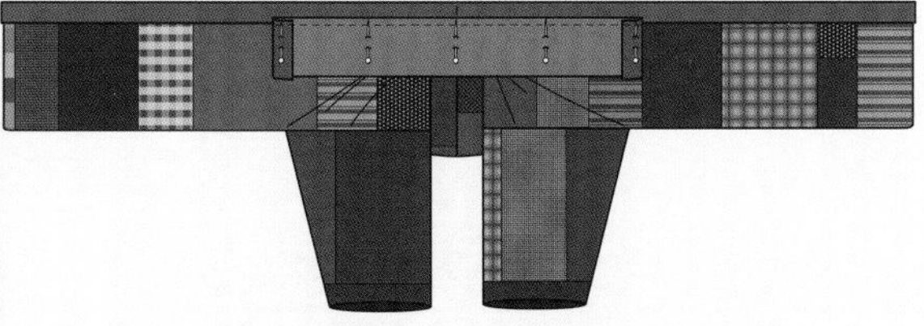
Fig 20

18 Add the collar cover: Not only does a collar cover reinforce the collar, but it can easily be replaced when it becomes worn. Fold the 30 x 6½in (76.2 x 16.5cm) collar cover piece in half so the short ends meet and crease to mark the centre. Line up the centre crease of the collar cover with the hanten's outer centre back seam and pin as shown by the central pin in Fig 20, overlapping the join of the collar and hanten by ⅜in (1cm). Fold over 2in (5cm) at each end of the collar cover. Hand sew the collar cover to the hanten, as shown in Fig 21.

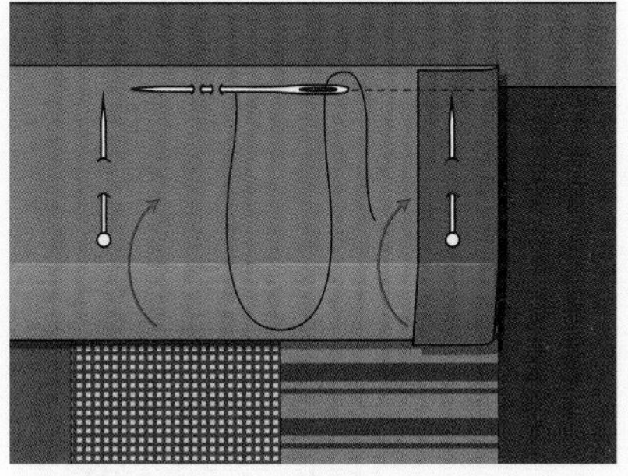
Fig 21

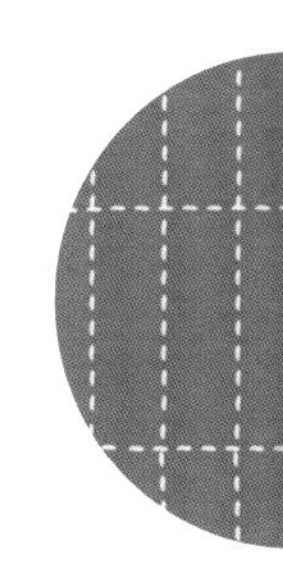

19 Hand sew the folded edge of the collar cover to the hanten. First fold the collar cover along its length into thirds approximately (like the collar itself), then fold the collar cover over the collar (Fig 22) and hand sew to the back of the collar, close to where it joins the hanten body.

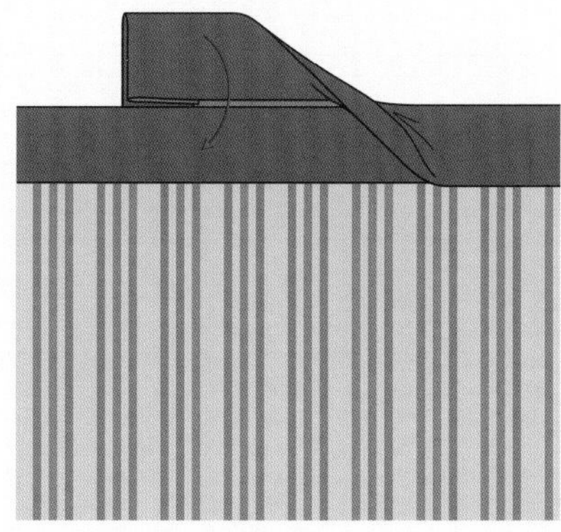

Fig 22

20 Add vertical lines of sashiko-style stitching to the hanten: Vertical rows of running stitch hold the outer and lining layers of the hanten together. Tack (baste) the outer fabric to the lining in horizontal lines across the body and sleeves before you start. Using cream sashiko thread, hand sew vertical lines of running stitch approx. 2in (5cm) apart across the body and sleeves, excluding the collar. The stitch lines do not need to be perfectly straight or evenly spaced – just follow lines in the stripes and checked patterns.

21 Add extra boro patches to the hanten: Hand sew a few patches to the hanten, to simulate wear and tear. Think about where the boro might get worn out first – shoulders, hip, front, elbows and cuffs are all likely places. This is a good opportunity to use up some tiny pieces of precious fabrics. Add patches in a variety of stitching styles and different threads, so it looks as if they have been added at different times, as if the hanten has been worn over several generations (see Techniques: Making Boro-Inspired Textiles).

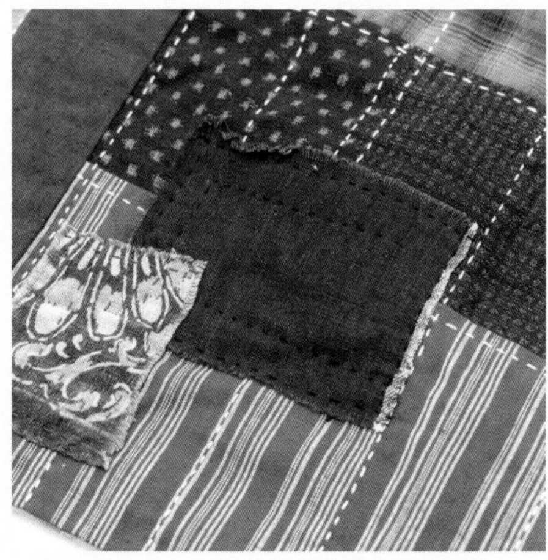

hinagata hanten

This miniature hanten is made in the style of a hinagata sewing sample (see How to Use This Book), with the same construction as the life-size jacket. The panels for the body are just 21 x 4½in (53.4 x 11.4cm) and for the sleeves, 6 x 41.2in (15.3 x 11.4cm) but seam allowances are life-sized (⅜in/1cm). To avoid too much bulk, I used a faux patchwork print for the body, fussy cut to get as many fabrics as possible showing in each panel, adding hand faux topstitching, so the panels appear to be pieced. The sleeves had to be handsewn to the body, and the sleeve wrist openings were slip stitched for *both* sleeves as the openings were too tiny for machine sewing.

The collar strip is 2½ x 25in (6.4 x 63.5cm), and the collar cover 2½ x 13½in (6.4 x 34.3cm), but a collar reinforcement is not needed. The lining has a 'seat reinforcement' added (see Yogi Quilt).

The finished jacket is displayed in a recessed frame. The backing board was covered in a plain linen-effect fabric held in place with double-sided tape and the hanging loop for the dowel is glued to the top of the board. The hanten hangs loose in the frame, so that you can turn it to see all the details. Put one sleeve on the dowel, thread the dowel through the loop, then slip the dowel through the other sleeve.

yogi quilt

The traditional *yogi* is a giant, thickly padded, kimono-shaped 'quilt', dating from c.1600, a time when commoners slept on straw. It is, in effect, an ancestor of the *kakebuton* (the top futon or quilt). It would have been used at night to provide a very warm cover, and rolled up during the day. I have reinvented the yogi as a snuggly sofa quilt, which has many similarities in its construction to the hanten jacket. To make the assembly of the yogi quilt easier, I have adapted the 'quilt as you go' concept to add a lighter-weight black wadding (batting) to a lining made from a patchwork of recycled kimono linings. The patchwork lining is edged with striped cotton that wraps around the hem and sleeve openings of the yogi outer. I boro-patched a favourite vintage plaid for the shoulder reinforcements and simplified the shape by removing the front overlap panels on the body. The underarm gussets give ease. The quilt layers are held in place with hand-tied sashiko thread knots.

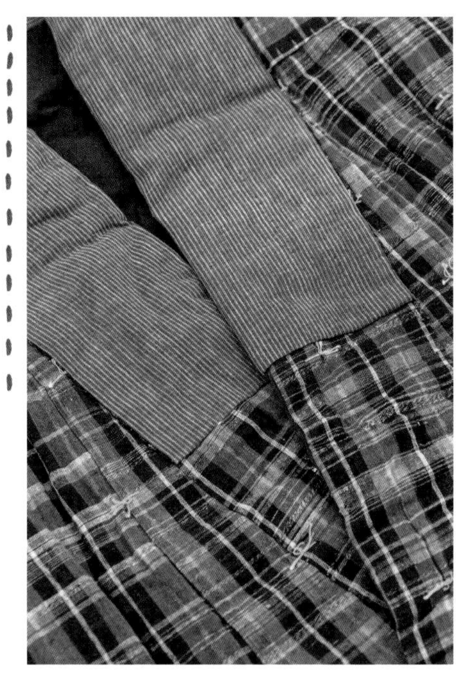

my inspiration

This photo shows a detail of the collar and front of an early twentieth-century yogi. The garment is relatively lightweight, made using a beautiful zanshi ori *(leftover thread weaving) fabric for the outer layer, with a lining pieced from plain indigo cotton. I love the ever-changing plaid, with its incredible number of indigo shades. The garment is tied at intervals with green thread to secure the layers – outer fabric, wadding (batting) and lining – in place.*

you will need

- Two pieces of cotton fabric 92 x 17in (234 x 43.2cm), for the upper panels of the body outer*
- Two pieces of cotton fabric 32 x 16in (81.3 x 40.6cm), for the sleeve outer
- Four pieces of cotton fabric 20 x 17in (50.8 x 43.2cm), for the lower panels of the body outer
- One piece of cotton plaid 50 x 14in (127 x 35.6cm), for the shoulder reinforcement panel**
- Four pieces of plain cotton 5in (12.7cm) square, for the sleeve gussets
- Assorted 6⅛in (15.6cm) wide strips of patchwork cotton or recycled cotton in various shades of blue, equivalent to approx. 2¾yd (2.5m) of 42in (106cm) wide fabric, for the lining
- One 14 x 10½in (35.5 x 26.5cm) piece of patchwork cotton or recycled cotton, for the seat patch
- Four pieces of striped cotton 11 x 17in (27.9 x 43.2cm), for the lower body edge
- Two pieces of striped cotton 13 x 32in (33 x 81.3cm), for the sleeve edge
- One piece of striped cotton 79 x 8¼in (200 x 20.9cm), for the collar
- One piece of cotton 43 x 8¼in (109 x 20.9cm), for the collar cover
- Co-ordinating fabric scraps for any necessary boro patching repairs
- Black cotton-blend wadding (batting), slightly larger than the lining panels: two pieces 158 x 18in (401 x 45.7cm), for the body; two pieces 33 x 17in (83.8 x 43.2cm), for the sleeves***
- 87yd (80m) fine sashiko thread in black
- 44yd (40m) medium sashiko thread in turquoise
- Oddments of fine sashiko thread in various colours for boro patching
- Machine sewing thread
- Basic sewing kit (see Tools and Materials)

**I used a piece of handwoven Thai fabric for the body panels. If you are using a handmade fabric, it is advisable to preshrink it by washing at 40°C before cutting to size.*

***This can be shorter, so long as it is long enough to cover the sleeve/body seams.*

****I used black wadding (batting) as it is less likely to show against the dark fabrics if it beards through the finished yogi. If you are using lighter fabrics, a natural wadding (batting) can be used.*

IMPORTANT NOTES ON GARMENT CONSTRUCTION

Seams are ⅜in (1cm) throughout, unless stated otherwise, and machine-sewn seams are recommended for strength. Start and finish all seams with a few reverse stitches.

If your sewing machine has a straight stretch stitch option, use that in preference to regular straight stitching for a more flexible seam – the weight of the yogi will put quite a lot of strain on the seams when worn! If you do choose to hand sew the garment, use half backstitch (see Techniques: Traditional Boro Stitches).

The wadding (batting) is captured in the seams as the lining is assembled and then sewn into the yogi. To avoid excessive bulk in the seams, use a small pair of scissors to carefully trim away the wadding (batting) within the seam allowance after each construction seam (see Fig 1), cutting about 1⁄16in (1.5mm) from the stitched seam.

The yogi is a fairly complex project, so please take your time and don't rush.

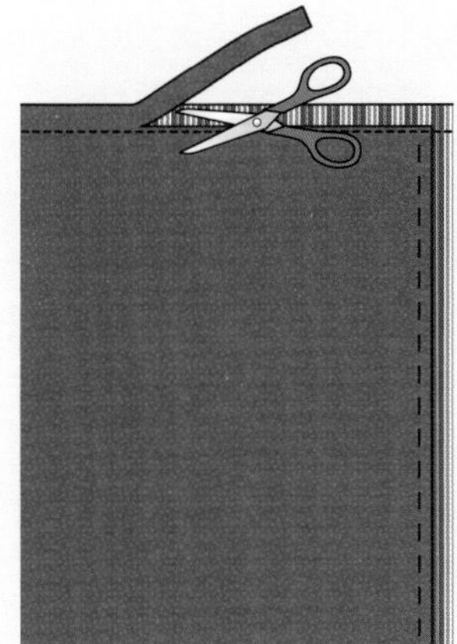
Fig 1

Fig 2: Piecing for yogi lining

1 Make the lining panels: Cut your assorted recycled fabrics into a variety of lengths, all 6⅛in (15.6cm) wide and, if necessary, add boro patches to the back of any that have small holes (see Techniques: Making Boro-Inspired Textiles – Raw-edge patch appliqué). Machine or hand sew your prepared fabrics into simple strip patchwork lengths (see Techniques: Patchwork for Boro), randomly mixing up the different fabrics as much as possible. These will be used to make the body lining and sleeve panels in step 2: for the body, you will need six strips measuring 136 x 6⅛in (345.5 x 15.5cm); for the sleeves, you will need four strips measuring 32 x 6⅛in (81.3 x 15.5cm)*. Press the patchwork seams towards what will be the bottom edges of the panels (note that the yogi has no shoulder seams).

**If you prefer, the body and sleeve lining panels can be made from single pieces of fabric: 136 x 17in (345.5 x 43.2cm) for each body lining panel and 32 x 11½in (81.3 x 29.2cm) for each sleeve.*

2 Pin and machine sew three of the longer strip patchwork lengths together to make each body lining panel. Pin and machine sew two of the shorter strip patchwork lengths together to make each sleeve lining panel.

3 To complete the piecing of the yogi lining, pin and machine sew one 11 x 17in (27.9 x 43.2cm) piece of striped cotton to each end of the body panels, and one 13 x 32in (33 x 81.3cm) piece of striped cotton to one side of each sleeve lining (see Fig 2).

The striped fabric will be wrapped around the lower hem and sleeve edges of the yogi quilt, so the lining panels are larger than the outer body and sleeve panels.

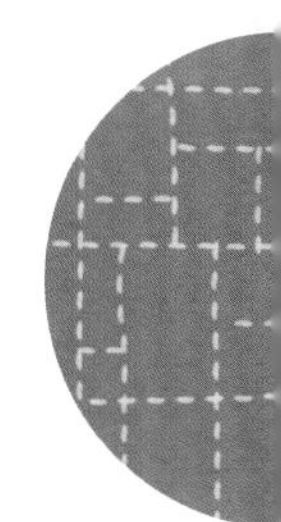

4 Layer and stitch the body lining panels to the wadding (batting): Lay one of the body wadding (batting) pieces front (fluffier) side down and smooth the first body lining panel over it, right side up. The wadding (batting) will be slightly larger than the lining panel. Use a long ruler to check that the long patchwork seams are straight. Tack (baste) approx. ⅛in (3mm) from the edge all around the lining panel, and add a second line of tacking (basting) about 1in (2.5cm) from the edge.

5 Using a small ⅛in (3mm) running stitch on top and a longer stitch around ⅜–½in (1–1.3cm) underneath, hand quilt in the ditch along all the patchwork seams with the fine black sashiko thread (see Techniques: Patchwork for Boro). This will hold the lining to the wadding (batting) so that the finished yogi isn't completely reliant on the tied knots to hold the layers together. It is easier to do this in the same way as tacking (basting), with the lining and wadding (batting) flat on a table (see Techniques: Running Stitch). Add two extra lines of stitching across the striped fabric sections at the ends, 3in (7.6cm) from the last seam and the same distance from the panel end.

6 Repeat steps 4 and 5 for the second body lining panel, then trim the edge of the wadding (batting) to match the edge of the panels.

7 Cut the collar neck shaping in the body lining panels: Refer to hanten jacket, step 2.

8 Machine sew the centre back seam on the body lining panels: Refer to hanten jacket, step 3.

9 Add the seat patch to the body lining: Turn under ½in (1.3cm) all around the seat patch piece and press to hold the edge in place. Pin the seat patch in place as a reinforcement across the centre back seam (Fig 3), positioning it 26in (66cm) from the bottom edge of the lining, and hand sew using a hem stitch first, followed by running stitch as described in step 5 ¼in (6mm) from the edge.

10 Layer and stitch the sleeve lining panels to the wadding (batting): Make sure one of the long edges of the wadding (batting) is cut perfectly straight. Lay the first of the sleeve wadding pieces front (fluffier) side down. Position the first sleeve lining section right side up on top of the wadding so that the straight edge of the wadding (batting) is 6in (15.2cm) from the edge of the striped fabric, as shown in Fig 4. This unpadded section will be folded back later to form the sleeve edge. Smooth the sleeve panel over the lining. Quilt the layers together as you did for the body panels (see steps 4 and 5), this time adding extra lines of quilting along the striped fabric approx. ½in (1.3cm), 2in (5cm) and 4in (10.2cm) from the edge of the wadding (batting). Tack (baste) approx. ⅛in (3mm) from the edge along the other three sides, and add a second line of tacking (basting) about 1in (2.5cm) from the edge (see Fig 4). Trim the edge of the wadding (batting) to match the edge of the panels on these sides.

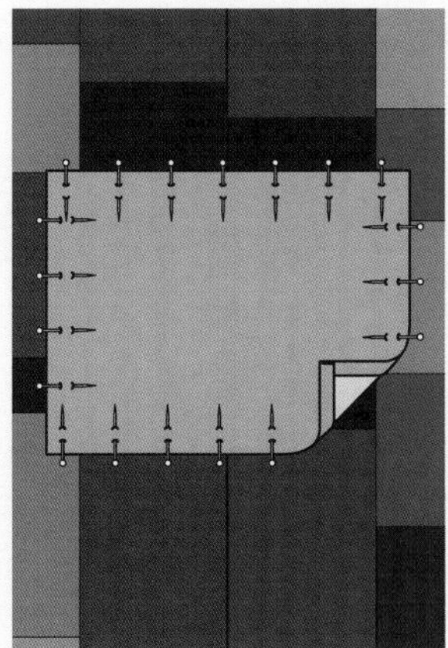

Fig 3

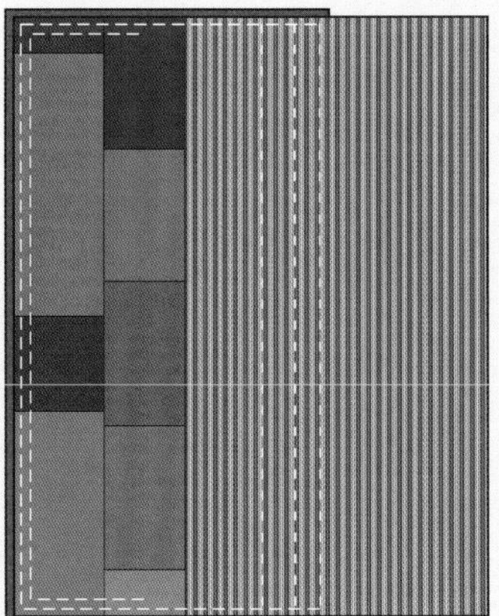

Fig 4

11 Assemble the sleeve linings: The sleeve gussets are sewn in three stages, in a Y-shaped seam, so two adjacent sides of the squares are attached to the sleeve and the other two are attached to the body (later in step 12). Draw a diagonal line in opposite corners on two of the 5in (12.7cm) sleeve gusset squares (Fig 5a). Pin one square to the body edge of one of the sleeve lining panels (Fig 5b), and machine sew from the edge of the square to the diagonal line (note that the sleeves are shown upside down in Figs 5b–5d, for ease of construction). Remove the pins. Fold the sleeve lining in half, right sides together, so that the lower edges of the sleeve lining match. Now attach the gusset square to the other lower sleeve lining edge (Fig 5c). From the end of the gusset panel stitching, finish sewing the seam along the lower edge of the sleeve lining, pinning and machine sewing from the corner of the sleeve gusset to the open end of the sleeve (Fig 5d). Repeat this step for the second sleeve lining.

12 Machine sew the body lining side seams and insert the sleeve linings: The body lining side seams are machine sewn in the same way as the hanten jacket side seams (see Hanten Jacket, step 5), leaving an opening of 17¾in (45cm) from the top of the shoulder fold for the sleeves. Turn the sleeve linings right side out, so that the patchwork fabric is on the outside. Flip the sleeve gussets out at the lower edge of the sleeves, as shown in Fig 6, and check this against the unsewn sleeve opening, which should be ⅜in (1cm) less than the measurement from the top fold of the sleeve to the sleeve gusset point. Mark the top of the shoulder and the top of the sleeve with pins to match up later. Insert the sleeve linings (see Hanten Jacket, step 6). Note that the sleeve gusset needs pinning to and stitching to the body lining with the same Y-shaped seam, so start pinning one side of the gusset first and work up towards the shoulder fold, as shown in Fig 7.

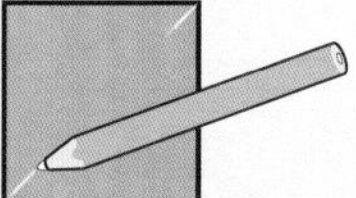

Fig 5a

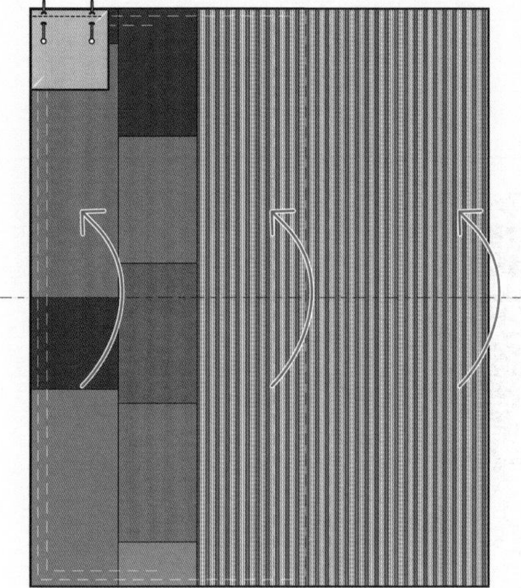

Fig 5b

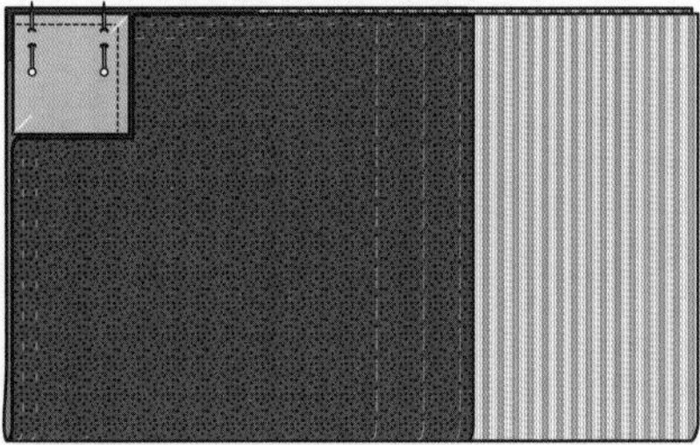

Fig 5c

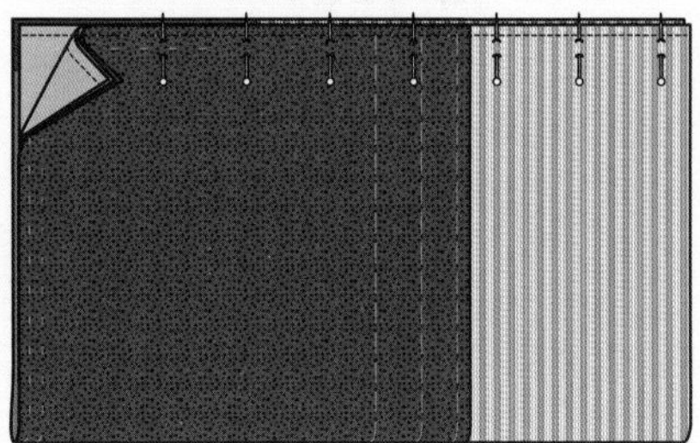

Fig 5d

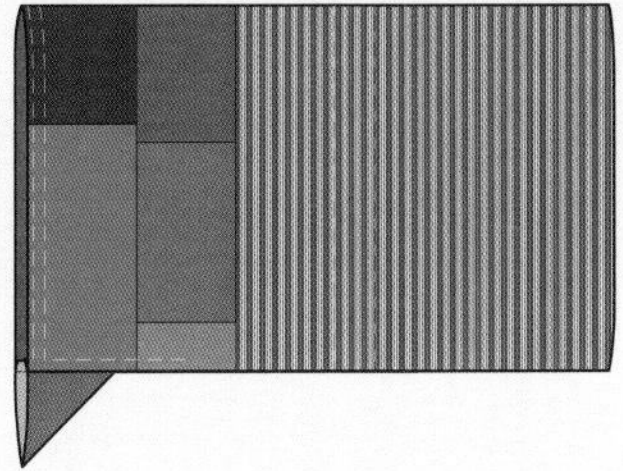

Fig 6

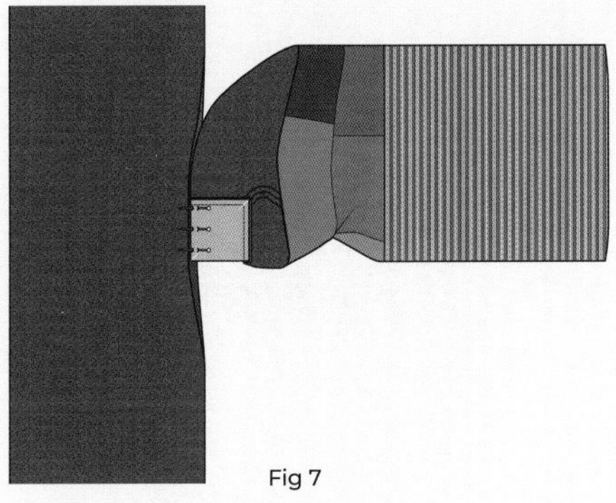

Fig 7

Fig 8

13 Make and assemble the body outer panels: Machine sew one 20 x 17in (50.8 x 43.2cm) lower panel to each end of the 92 x 17in (234 x 43.2cm) upper panels, and press the seams towards the lower panels. Cut the collar neck shaping and sew the centre back seam as you did for the lining (see steps 7 and 8).

14 Tack (baste) the shoulder reinforcement panel to the body outer: I used a vintage plaid for my shoulder reinforcement panel so first I made some small boro patch repairs that were required (see Techniques: Making Boro-Inspired Textiles – Reverse appliqué). Turn under ⅜in (1cm) all around the shoulder reinforcement panel and pin it to the body, centring it on the shoulder section. Tack (baste) it in place to within 2in (5cm) of the sides of the body panel, leaving the ends of the shoulder reinforcement panel hanging loose for now. Using the body panel's collar neckline cut as a guide, cut the shoulder reinforcement in the same way and tack (baste) it to the body around the curve. Now fold the ends of the shoulder reinforcement back over the body panels, so that they are out of the way while the sleeves are sewn to the body, and tack (baste) in place as shown in Fig 8; note that this diagram also includes the sleeve panels laid flat to show their position relative to the shoulder reinforcement.

15 Make the sleeve outer panels, sew the side seams and sew the sleeves to the body outer: Make each sleeve using one piece of cotton fabric 32 x 16in (81.3 x 40.6cm) plus one 5in (12.7cm) gusset square, following the instructions for the lining in step 11. Machine sew the side seams and insert the sleeves to the body, following the instructions for the lining in step 12.

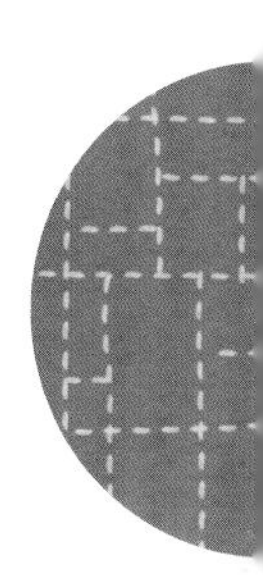

16 Sew the shoulder reinforcement panel to the body outer: Undo the tacking (basting) stitches used to hold the shoulder reinforcement panel out of the way when the sleeves were sewn on, and pin the ends over the top of the sleeves. Using fine black sashiko thread and hem stitch, hand sew the edges of the shoulder reinforcement panel to the sleeves. Using medium turquoise sashiko thread, stitch a line of sashiko-style running stitch all the way around the panel ¼in (6mm) from the edge, going through both the panel and the body fabric, then stitch several rows of running stitch across the reinforcement panel, following lines in the weave (Fig 9).

17 Sew the body outer to the lining: Up to this point, we have been working on constructing the outer and the lining independently of each other and Figs 10 and 11 show how each looks at this stage, with the lining (Fig 10) so much longer at the bottom edge and at the sleeves than the outer (remember that the striped cotton fabric of the lining will be wrapped around to the front of the outer). It is now time to join the lining to the outer, which we shall now refer to as the yogi. With right sides facing, pin the bottom edges of the yogi and the lining together, then machine sew. Make sure the centre back seams are pointing to the left of the yogi, and the two side seams are pointing to the right. Press the bottom seam downwards.

18 Continuing with right sides facing, pin the front edge of the lining and the yogi fabric together along one side, starting at the collar cut and working towards the bottom edge. Keep the edges flat so that you don't ease more lining to the outer fabric or vice versa. When you reach the bottom edge, the 'hemline' will fall into place naturally. Pin the remaining front edge in the same way, and check that the horizontal seam between the yogi and lining falls in the same place along the right and left front edges. Then, starting from the lower edge each time, machine sew the lining to the yogi, stitching approx. 42in (107cm) up from the bottom edge.

Fig 9

Fig 10: The yogi lining

Fig 11: The yogi outer

Fig 12

Fig 13

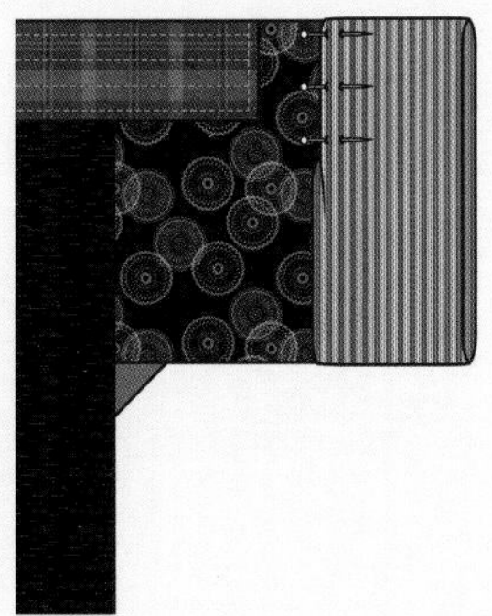

Fig 14

19 Working through the unsewn portion of the upper front edges, carefully turn the yogi and its lining right side out, making sure that the bottom front corners are fully turned out. Now push the lining through the sleeves until the striped fabric comes out at the sleeve openings (these will be finished in step 20). Referring to the hanten jacket, step 11, stitch the yogi seam allowances to the lining seam allowances; for the side seams, start stitching around 2in (5cm) below the sleeve gussets. Refer to Fig 12 for how the yogi should look at this point in its construction.

20 Finish the sleeve openings: Working on one sleeve at a time, slide your hand in between the lining and the outer fabric and take hold of both the lining and outer seam allowances. With both the seam allowances pointing towards the front of the yogi, stitch the seam allowances together, referring to hanten jacket, step 11; start stitching the seams around 1in (2.5cm) from the sleeve gussets, finishing at the end of the outer sleeve fabric (Fig 13).

21 It is now time to fold the striped fabric of the lining back over the outer sleeve fabric on each seam, allowing ¼in (6mm) of wadding (batting) to roll back at the edge, to make the edge a little thicker. Use the second version of the edge, stitch to hand sew the sleeve opening in place (see Techniques: Traditional Boro Stitches – Edge stitch). Smooth the rest of the striped fabric back over the outer sleeve to create a deep cuff. Turn under the edge of the cuff by ½in (1.3cm) evenly all around and pin it in place (Fig 14); then hand hem stitch the folded edge of the lining to the outer fabric all round. Take care that the lining and outer sleeve fabrics don't bunch up.

22 Attach the collar and collar cover: The collar secures the outer and lining layers of the yogi along the upper front edges and around the back of the neck. On the front of the yogi, mark a line on each side of the collar neck shaping for 4in (10.2cm) parallel to the front opening, then draw a line sloping down to the point at the top of where the lining and the outer fabric are sewn together (see Fig 15). Apart from this sloping direction, the collar and collar cover are added to the yogi following the same method used for the hanten jacket (refer to hanten jacket, steps 12–19). To prevent the collar from becoming too bulky at the front, carefully remove the wadding (batting) from the back of the lining fabric before folding the layers into the collar. Ladder or slip stitch the ends of the collar cover down onto the collar.

23 Tie the layers with sashiko thread: Using the turquoise sashiko thread (or another colour of your choice), complete the yogi by hand tying: stitch lengths of the thread through the fabric layers at regular intervals and tie each in a reef or square knot (as shown in Fig 16*), working your way all over the quilt. Lay the yogi on a table and slide a large cutting mat (or thin chopping board or similar) inside, to ensure you don't accidentally tie the front of the yogi to the back! First, mark the position of the ties – your fabric may have a line or a repeat that you can use to help you to do this. For my yogi quilt, I used a 4½in (11.4cm) wide quilter's ruler to space the ties on the back and the front, following two vertical lines in the main outer fabric, which were approx. 7in (17.8cm) apart (see Fig 17). After these ties were done, extra ties were added in between, 3½in (8.9cm) horizontally and 2½in (6.4cm) vertically from the previous ones. Orange glass-headed pins were used to temporarily mark the position of all the ties on the busily patterned katazome-style print used for the lower panels and sleeves, as shown in Fig 17. If you prefer, mark all the tie positions on one half of the yogi front before starting to stitch the ties, but you will need quite a lot of pins. On the shoulder reinforcement, the ties are at the same intervals across the yogi but the vertical spacing changes so the ties are equidistant between the turquoise sashiko rows. On the sleeves, the spacing is changed slightly, keeping the vertical spacing from the body but moving the ties to suit the edge of the shoulder reinforcement. There are no ties at the very top of the shoulder or on the striped hem and sleeve opening fabrics. Tie both sides of the front and the front of the sleeves, then turn the yogi over and tie the back and the back of the sleeves. Once all the ties have been made, your yogi quilt is complete.

**It is easier and more economical with your thread to leave the needle on the end of the remaining thread while tying the knot.*

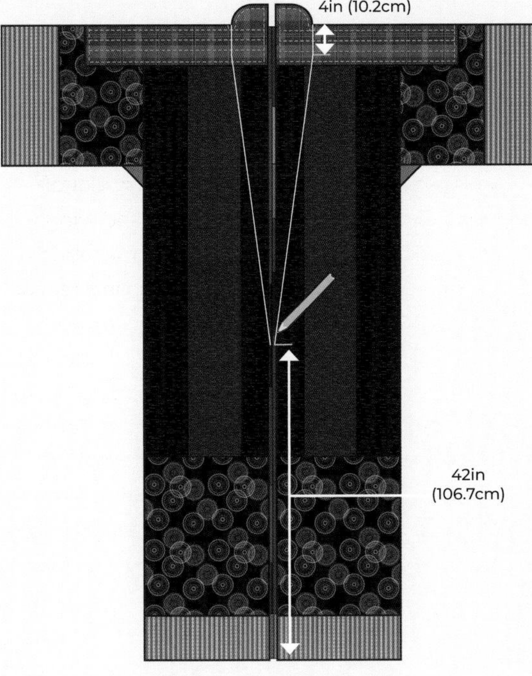

Fig 15

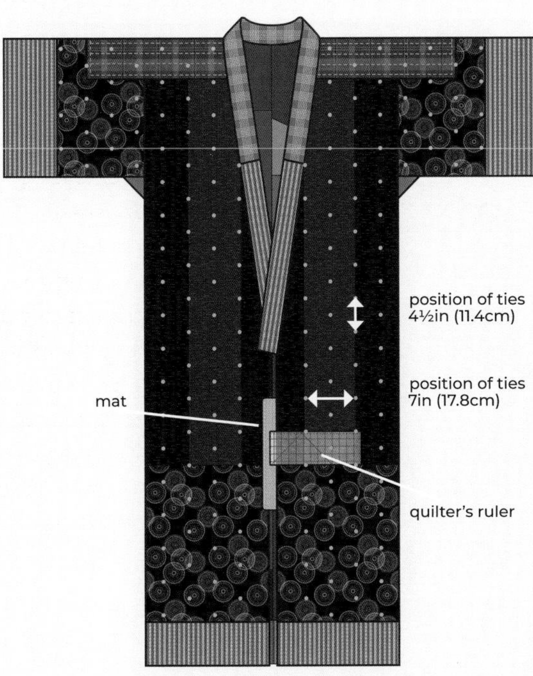

Fig 17

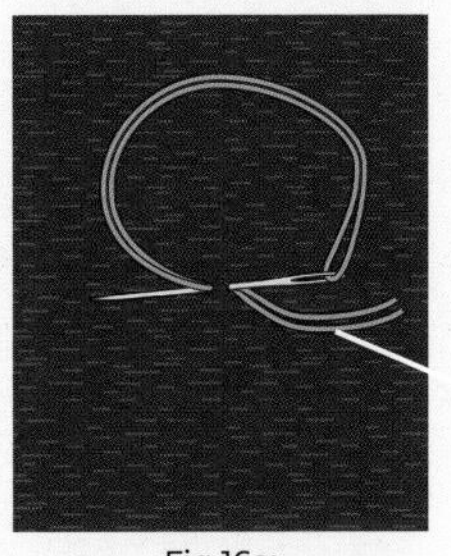

Fig 16a:

Take a scant ¼in (5mm) backstitch through all layers

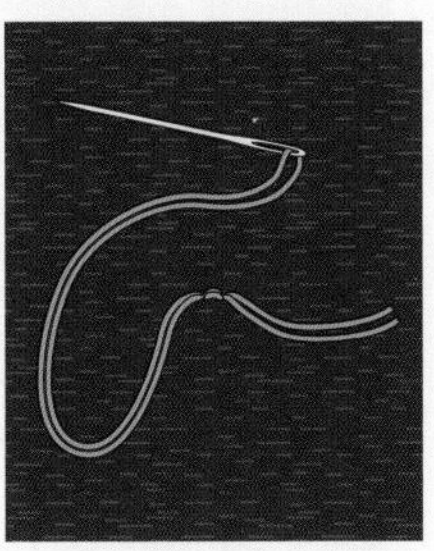
Fig 16b:
Pull stitch tight

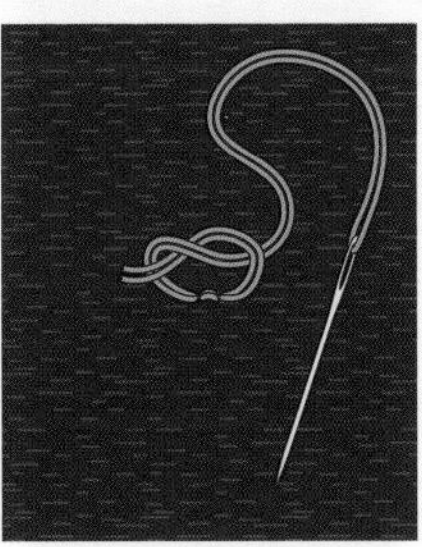

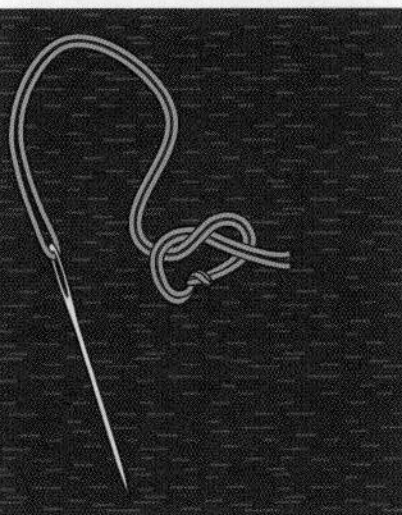
Fig 16c:
Tie tight reef knot with thread ends

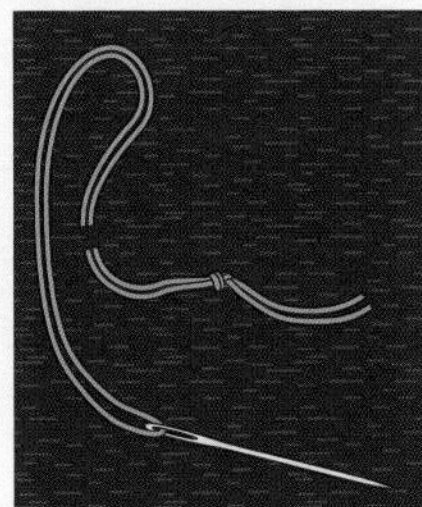
Fig 16d:
Trim ends to approx. 1in (2.5cm)

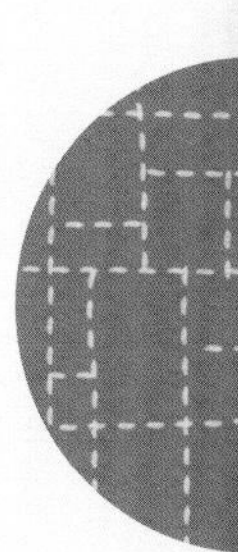

The patchworked lining gives the inside of the yogi added interest and is a great way to use up lots of smaller pieces of many indigo blue fabrics.

Turquoise sashiko thread was chosen for the ties because it coordinated beautifully with the bright blue touches in the antique plaid fabric.

hinagata yogi

This miniature yogi is made in the style of a hinagata sewing sample (see How to Use This Book), so it has a similar construction to the larger yogi quilt, but measures just 10in (25.4cm) long. The linings are cut as one piece, without patchwork, to reduce bulk, so the body lining pieces were 22 x 3in (55.8 x 7.6cm) and the sleeve linings 6 x 3¾in (15.2 x 9.5cm). The main body panels are 15in x 3in (38.1 x 7.6cm), the lower panels 3½ x 3in (8.9 x 7.6cm) and the sleeves 6 x 2½in (15.2 x 6.4cm). Seam allowances are the same (⅜in/1cm). The sleeves are handsewn to the body and the sleeve gussets omitted. The collar strip is 2½ x 12in (6.4 x 30.5cm) and the collar cover 2½ x 6½in (6.4 x 16.5cm).

The finished yogi is displayed in a recessed frame and hangs loose so you can turn it around to see all the details. I have used the same frame size as that used for the hinagata hanten, so that you could ring the changes and display them in turn in the same frame, or display the back of the miniature rather than the front view.. For more details about the framing, refer to hinagata hanten.

box cushion

A box cushion for a favourite chair or stool looks lovely made from an assortment of traditional checks and stripes pieced together as a foundation for patches you've saved for that special project. Japanese *zabuton* (large floor cushions) sometimes have the same boxed-out corner detail. This cushion cover is made from a long strip of pieced and patched fabrics, hemmed and folded to overlap on the underside, but with just enough of a gap for you to be able to easily remove the specially made cushion pad when it comes to laundering. And, by making the pad as well as the cushion, you can resize it for use as a seat cushion for any chair or stool with a rectangular or square seat. The use of checked and striped fabrics means that stitching a grid is easy – just follow the lines in the weave.

my inspiration

This child's kimono, made from antique handwoven plaids and stripes, was made by Japanese fabric collector, Izuho Horiuchi, in the last quarter of the twentieth century. It was probably made for display, as it looks unworn. It is a treasure trove of weaves; Horiuchi selected some very well-preserved patches in a variety of scales, in assorted shades of natural indigo, and combined them in an asymmetric arrangement.

you will need

- One piece of plain fabric 15¼ x 37¾in (38.7 x 95.9cm), for the cushion pad*
- Assorted fabric scraps including checks and stripes, for the cushion cover**
- 109yd (100m) fine or medium sashiko thread in various colours
- Machine sewing thread to co-ordinate with patches***
- Stuffing, for cushion pad
- Basic sewing kit (see Tools and Materials)

**This makes a cushion pad with an approx. size of 15¾ x 11¾ x 2¾in (40 x 30 x 7cm), but you can easily adapt the size to fit your chair as outlined in step 1.*

***Approx 1½yd (1.37m) of 43¼in (110cm) wide fabric in total.*

****I have machine sewn the construction seams and patchwork but these can be handsewn using backstitch if you prefer.*

1 Calculate fabric requirements for your cushion: Starting with the cushion pad, note the width and length of the cushion you want to make (this will depend on the chair or stool you want the pad to be made to fit – see my working example, below). Add the proposed cushion depth (thickness) required to each measurement, to give you a rectangle or square size equivalent to one side of your cushion panel, including the boxed corner points. As the cushion pad is made from a continuous fabric strip, the shape you need to cut is like the top and bottom of the pad, joined side by side, with 1in (2.5cm) added to the total size to allow a ½in (1.3cm) seam allowance all round.

To determine the size of the patchwork foundation strip required for the cushion cover, add ¾in (2cm) to the width of the cushion pad fabric measurements for ease, and 3in (7.6cm) to the total length for the overlap underneath the cushion cover. If your cushion is significantly larger than mine, add 4in (10.2cm) for a more generous cover overlap.

My working example: I wanted my cushion to fit a Tendo Mokko 'butterfly stool', a popular modern mid-century Japanese design, so it needed to measure 15¾ long x 11¾in (40 x 30cm) wide. For comfort, 2¾in (7cm) seemed an adequate thickness:

Length: 15¾ + 2¾ = 18½in (40 + 7= 47cm)
Width: 11¾ + 2¾ = 14½in (30 +7 = 37cm)

Double the length, then add 1in (2.5cm) to both the length and the width to account for the seam allowances; this gives you the total amount of fabric you need for the cushion pad.

For the cushion cover, I added ¾in (2cm) to the shortest measurement and 4in (10.2cm) to the longest measurement, so the finished size of the cushion cover panel is 41 x 16in (104 x 40.6cm), including a 3in (7.6cm) overlap once the ends are hemmed (hemming takes up ½in (1.3cm) at each end).

Sketching out the shape of your cushion will make calculating the correct sizes easier.

2 Make the cushion pad: Fold the cushion pad fabric in half with right sides together, so that the short ends meet, and pin in place. Machine stitch with a ½in (1.3cm) seam allowance, leaving a 4in (10.2cm) gap in the middle of the seam (Fig 1). Press the seam to one side.

Start and finish machine-sewn seams with a few backstitches throughout this project.

Fig 1

Fig 2

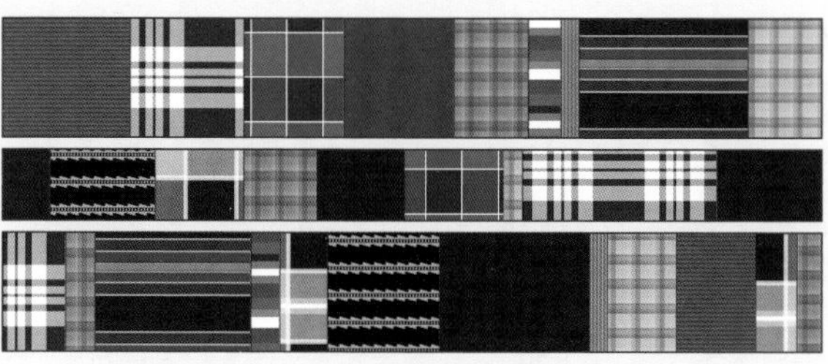

Fig 3

3 Fold the cushion pad fabric so that the seam you have just sewn is in the centre. Pin, then machine sew along each open edge, being sure to stitch right to the very ends (Fig 2). Press seam to one side.

4 Box-out the corners of the seams just sewn (see Techniques: Making Up Projects), machine sewing 1⅜in (3.5cm) up from the corner point, then trimming the corner point to leave a ½in (1.3cm) seam allowance.

5 Turn the cushion pad fabric right side out through the gap in the central seam. Use the stuffing to stuff the cushion pad evenly, then ladder stitch or slipstitch the turning gap closed.

6 **Make the cushion cover panel:** Start by making the patchwork foundation for the cushion cover panel by machine sewing your selected fabric patches together into two or three strips (Fig 3). Finish each seam with zigzag stitch (or a hand whip stitch) as you go, to keep the back of the panel fairly neat and to stop the seams from fraying when the cushion is in use. Press seams to one side, then topstitch along each seam with a handsewn running stitch.

7 Sew your patchwork strips together to give you an overall patchwork piece the size required as determined in step 1 – mine measures 41 x 16in (104 x 40.6 cm) (Fig 4). Press and topstitch these seams also (see step 6).

8 Hem both short ends of the cushion cover panel: turn under ¼in (6mm) twice and hem stitch in place. You can work an additional line of running stitch along the hems to reinforce the edges.

9 Add appliqué patches on top of the patchwork panel, turning the edges on some and leaving the edges raw on others. For extra texture, work a few darned areas too (see Techniques: Making Boro-Inspired Textiles). Note that the central 26in (66cm) of the panel will be visible at the top and sides when the cushion is finished, so concentrate on this area for now (extra patches can be added later) and be sure to place your favourite patches so that they will be visible on the finished cover. Think about where the cushion is likely to become worn when in use, such as the edges and top. Add some extra darning or sashiko patches to the parts that will become the edges. Stitch patches down individually, then add long lines of running stitch going across the panel in both directions.

10 Make the cushion cover: First, finish the long edges of the patched patchwork panel with machine zigzag stitch (or hand whip stitch). With the prepared panel right side facing up, fold the short ends over until they overlap in the centre by 2in (5cm), as shown in Fig 5. Keeping this towards the centre of the cushion, pin the long edges together and machine or hand stitch backstitch, as shown by the dashed lines.

11 Box out the corners of the cushion cover in the same way as the cushion pad, referring to step 4.

12 Turn the cushion cover right side out. A few extra patches can be added, bridging the side seams. Once again, think about where the cushion might wear when in use. Insert the cushion pad to finish your cushion.

Fig 4

Fig 5

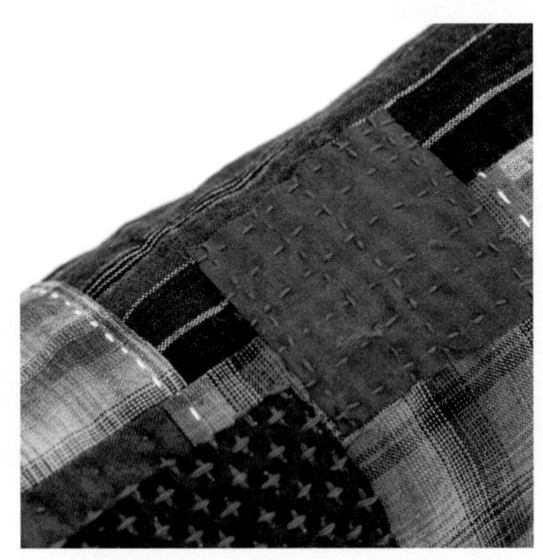

giant pincushion

A mini version of the box cushion makes a generously sized pincushion that will be very useful for your adventures in boro. Make a strip of boro-inspired patchwork, adding a few appliqué patches, and assemble it following the cushion pad instructions. A strip measuring 16 x 6in (40.6 x 15.2cm) will make a large pincushion to hold a lot of pins (I recycled two of the waste pieces left from trimming the hanten jacket sleeves). Box-out the corners in the same way as for the larger cushion, but stitch only ¾in (2cm) from the corner point, or less if you are making a slightly smaller pincushion.

table runner

I have used a pair of worn tie-dyed trousers as the basis for the foundation panel of this table runner, unpicking them to use many of the component parts to create interesting shapes to the background. Playing with the idea of old boro having a fairly neat front and a patched back, this runner has been designed to be fully reversible, presenting a different look depending on which side is up. Here, the patched side is shown, with its harmonious selection of plaids, stripes and *kasuri* (ikat) fabrics. Blue-and-white variegated sashiko thread gives a subtle effect. The blanket-stitched reverse appliqué circles and chain-stitch spirals were inspired by contemporary boro-style stitching. Turn over the runner and a more minimal design will be revealed: this side has no patches, just more stitching and reverse appliqué in variegated sashiko thread.

my inspiration

This old kimono, aptly described as sodenashi *(sleeveless) when I bought it, has lost both sleeves and collar, but gained an amazingly textured boro section around the lower half. From the outside, there is a selection of holes of different shapes and sizes, with large, random stitches in white thread, plus wavy lines of running stitch, while inside it has a beautiful assortment of fabric patches, including some very old hand weaves.*

you will need

- One pair of old cotton or linen trousers, plain or patterned*
- An assortment of small fabric scraps, including stripes and checks, up to 9in (22.8cm) wide
- 109yd (100m) of medium sashiko thread in yellow-and-green and blue-and-white variegated, cream and dark blue
- Basic sewing kit (see Tools and Materials)

**Alternatively, you can use several fabric pieces, equivalent to about 39in (1m) of 43 ¼ in (110cm) wide fabric.*

1 Choose your main pieces for the foundation backing panel: I unpicked my pair of tie-dye trousers completely, so I could use all the variety of the seams, the fades, and the worn areas when piecing my foundation backing panel. Pieces like the pockets and waistband had interesting shapes that could be cut up and used. Even the belt loops were unpicked and recycled. The edges of the backing panel will be folded over to the front by at least 4in (10.2cm) all around, so to make a table runner the same finished size as mine, that is 16 x 56in (40.6 x 142.2cm), the total measurement needs to be at least 24 x 64in (61 x 162.6cm). Start by choosing the largest pieces of fabric. You will be overlapping several pieces together to make the backing and it is easier to do this if the edges are fairly straight. I used the full length of two trouser legs, with the outer edge trimmed straight, and cut a shorter section from the front of the other leg to be placed at each end.

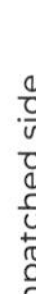

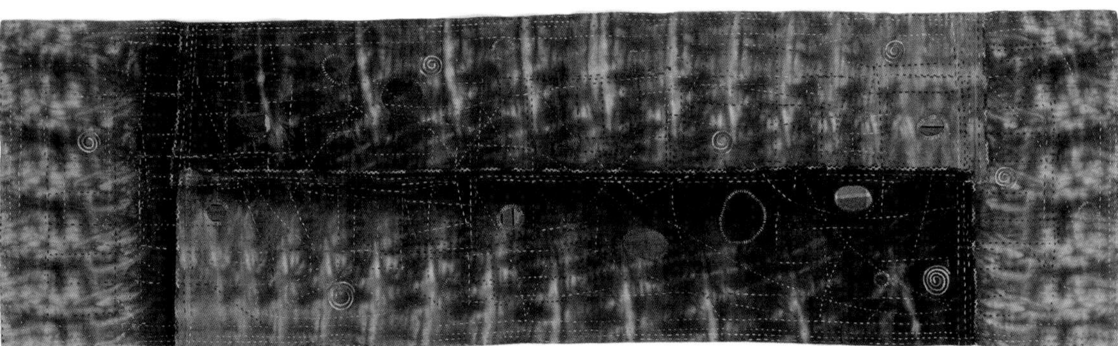

Unpatched side

Patched side

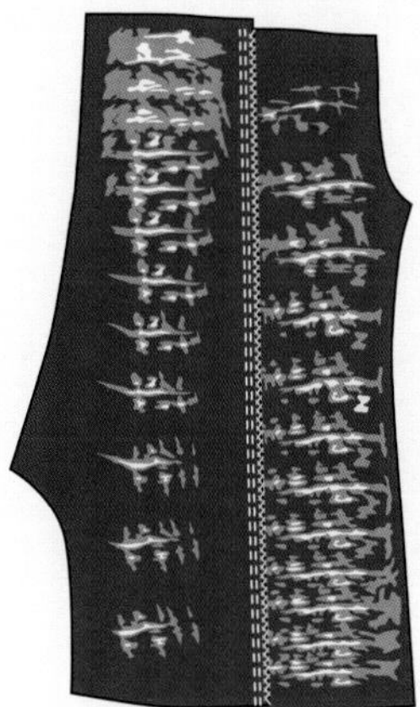

Fig 1

2 Piece the foundation backing panel: Overlap the long sides of the two longest pieces of fabric by about 1in (2.5cm), keeping them as flat as possible. Pin and, using the blue-and-white variegated sashiko thread, hand sew running stitch along the centre of the overlap (Fig 1 – the fabrics are shown with slight transparency so that the overlap is visible). Now hand sew herringbone stitch along the edge of the joined fabric pieces (see Techniques: Traditional Boro Stitches).

3 Take your shorter end pieces of fabric and overlap, pin and stitch as in step 2 (Fig 2). (Remember, there is no need to square off the sides of the fabrics – these will be folded into the table runner edges, creating an interesting effect where they are stitched in place.)

Fig 2

4 Mark out the table runner shape on the foundation backing panel: Place the foundation backing panel on your work surface with the herringbone stitch side facing up. Use a fabric marker to draw a rectangle 16 x 56in (40.6 x 142.2cm) for the shape of your table runner (you can adapt this size as you wish, but remember to allow approx. 4in (10.2cm) minimum all around for the turned edge). It is easiest to do this by measuring a set distance either side of the join that runs down the centre, for example, 7in (17.8cm) on one side and 9in (22.9cm) on the other. Extend the marked lines right out to the edges of the fabric (Fig 3 – the table runner shape is shown by the shaded area). Turn the panel over, so that the herringbone stitches are underneath, then fold the edges towards the centre, pressing along the marked lines, first along the sides and then along the ends.

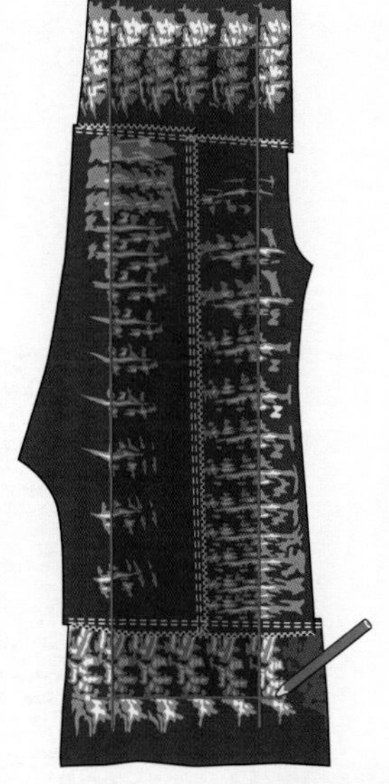

Fig 3

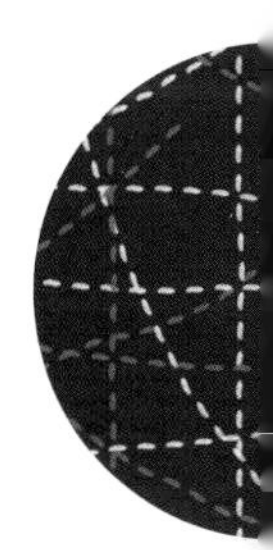

5 Make the mitred corners: Fold the corners in one by one on the diagonal, lining up along the pressed creases, as shown by the red line in Fig 4a. Fold the sides in along the red lines and press, as shown in Fig 4b. Fold the top edge downwards and the bottom edge upwards, so that the folded edges meet in the corners in neat mitres, as shown in Fig 4c. There is no need to trim any fabric away inside the mitre as it will lie quite flat, and do not worry that the width of the hem varies between the end and the side of the panel (this will be hidden when the raw edges are overlapped with the handsewn patches in steps 7 and 10). Pin and tack (baste) each mitred corner, then ladder stitch each corner mitre (see Techniques: Traditional Boro Stitches), starting at the corner and stitching inwards.

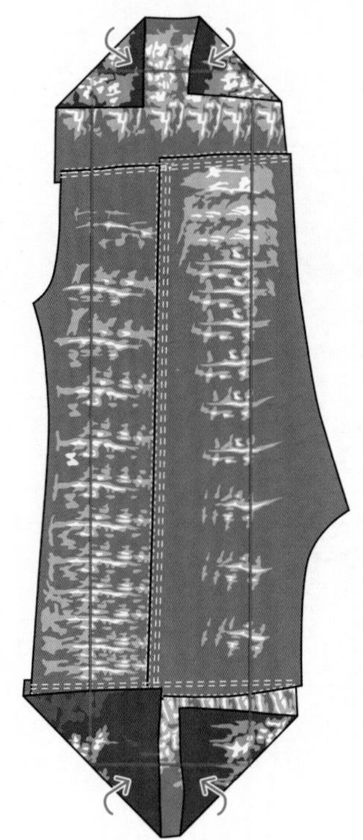

Fig 4a

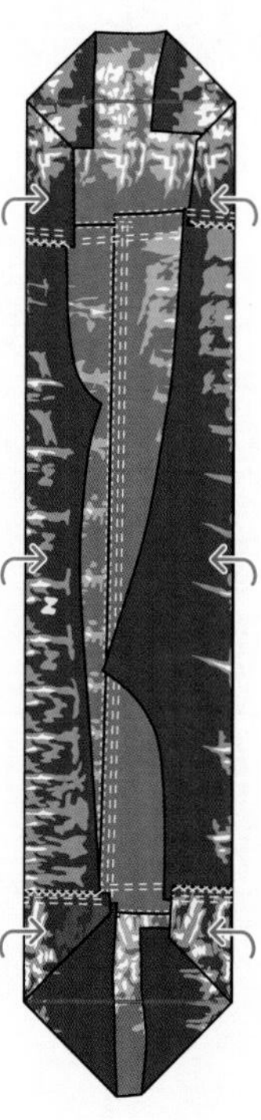

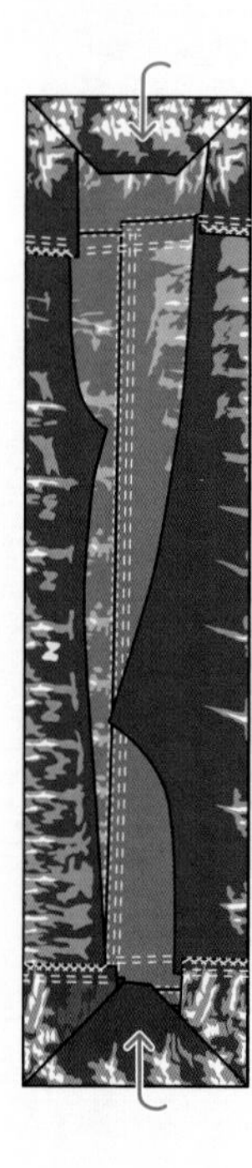

Fig 4b

Fig 4c

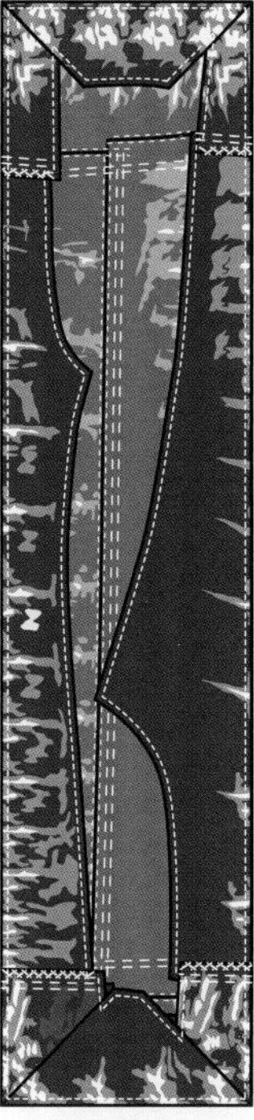

Fig 5

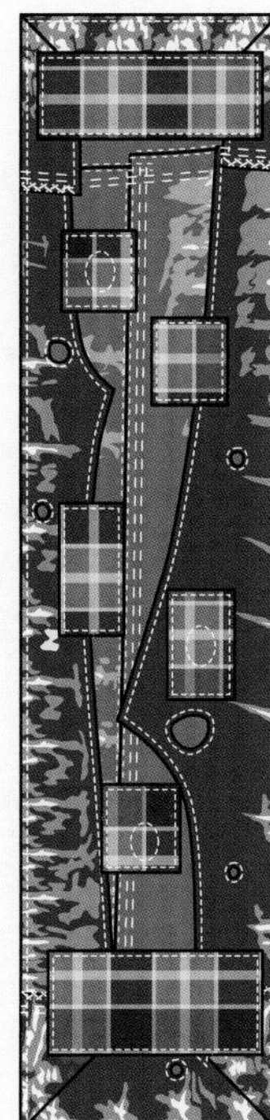

Fig 6

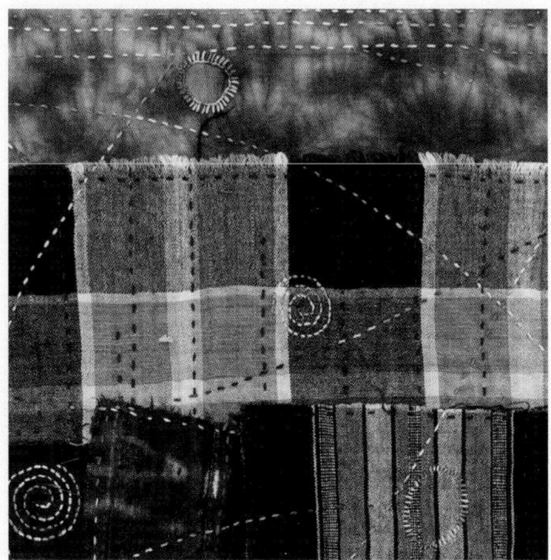

6 Complete the 'border': Pin the edge fold in place all around the panel. Hand sew running stitch through both layers about ⅛in (3mm) from the folded edge, using a variegated sashiko or similar thread (Fig 5). Hand sew running stitch to hold down the irregular raw edges of the pieced foundation backing panel. These stitching lines create interesting shapes on the other (unpatched) side of the panel.

7 Add the first patches: Position your most striking fabrics first (Fig 6). I cut up a large-scale check and put strips at each end of the runner and arranged squares and rectangles of varying size down the length, alternating them from side to side. When positioning the strips and patches, overlap the raw edges of the folded edge, and when you are happy with the arrangement, pin them in place. Using variegated and dark blue sashiko thread, hand sew the patches with running stitch worked around the edges only at this stage.

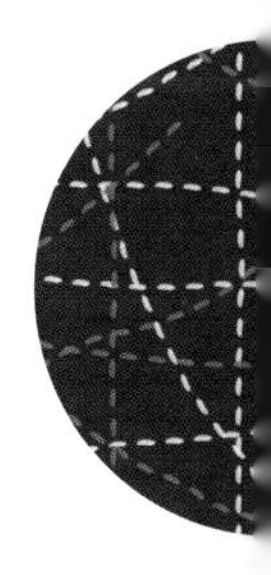

8 Make the reverse appliqué holes: Working from both sides of the table runner, cut out several small holes through whichever fabric is the topmost layer only (this may be a patch or the main fabric panel); I cut the holes freehand, so the sizes and shapes vary from circular to oval. Tack (baste) around each cut hole, ¼in (6mm) from the edge (see top two photos).

9 Hand sew around each cut-out shape using variegated sashiko thread, stitching some with appliqué hem stitch and some with blanket stitch. These stiches give an attractive effect on the unpatched side of the runner too, with the appliqué hem stitch resembling stem stitch and the blanket stitch making a series of short lines (see bottom photo).

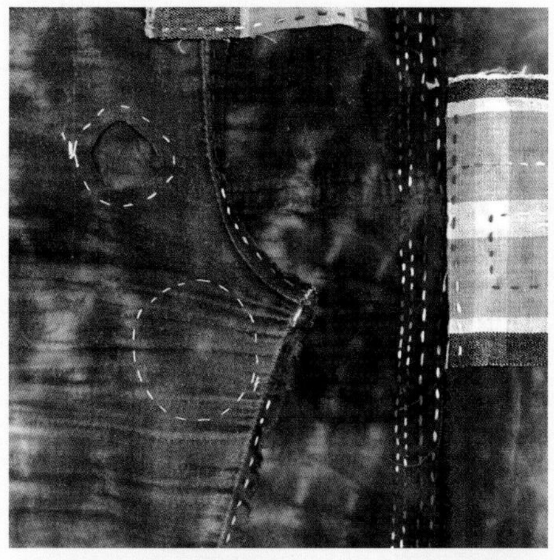

10 Add more patches: Continue adding patches as shown in Fig 7, stitching with variegated and cream and dark blue sashiko threads. Add some extra stitching within the patches previously applied, such as stitching back and forth or in a spiral, as well as to subsequent patches. Play with the arrangement until you like the effect. Some bolder fabrics, such as the yellow ochre scrim and the woven stripes, will look better cut up and placed in several different areas (if left as larger pieces they could dominate the other patches). Pin in place and stitch around the edge of each patch as before.

11 Now add more patches, as shown in Fig 8. This is a good point to start filling in spaces with less boldly patterned fabrics. I used more pieces cut from what remained of my tie-dyed trousers, including the pockets, pocket flaps and pieces from the waistband, to fill in areas where no patches were overlapping the raw edges of the panel border. Some of these patches have slightly curved edges or are placed at a slight angle, which makes the patch layout look lively. As the table runner is used and becomes more worn, extra patches and stitching can be added, of course.

12 Complete the finishing details: Work extra rows of running stitch around the table runner edges, or areas of darning or *hitomezashi* (see Techniques: Simple Sashiko). You might also want to add a few smaller patches, either to fill in plainer areas or to break up the long edges on the table runner ends. Add some small chain stitch spirals to the unpatched side to balance up the reverse appliqué holes (see Techniques: Modern Boro Stitches), first drawing the starting circles by freehand. It is a good idea to wash the table runner before use to fray the patch edges slightly.

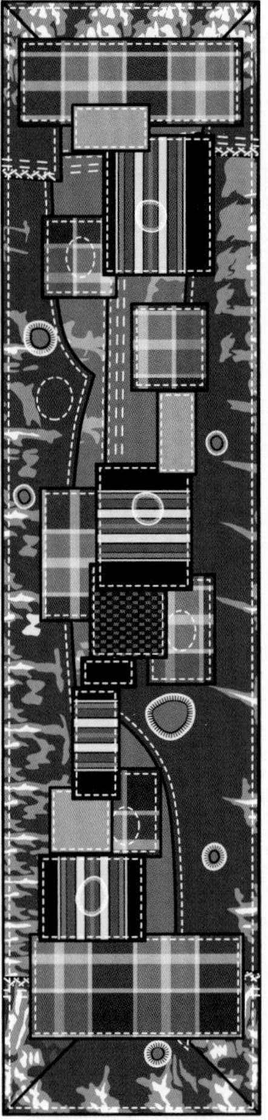

Fig 7

Fig 8

reversible bookmark

The same basic folding technique used to edge the table runner can be downsized to make a reversible bookmark. To avoid too much bulk, use fine sashiko thread, starting and finishing stitching without a knot (see Techniques: Stitching Boro), and choose fairly thin fabrics too. I used a 9 x 6in (22.9 x 15.2cm) strip, folding over about a 1in (2.5cm) border all around, mitring the corners as I went. With a finished size of 7 x 4in (17.8 x 10.2cm), the bookmark can usefully double up as a mug rug while you are reading! I added a treasured scrap of antique *katazome* (stencil dyed) cotton.

suppliers

Susan Briscoe Designs (UK)
www.susanbriscoe.com

Japan Crafts (UK)
www.japancrafts.co.uk

Textile Traders (UK)
www.textiletraders.co.uk

Marita Rolin (Sweden)
www.maritarolin.se

BeBe Bold Europe (France)
bebebold.eu

BeBe Bold (Australia)
www.bebebold.com

Indigo Niche (Australia)
www.indigoniche.com

Wabi-Sabi Designs (Australia)
wabi-sabi.com.au

KimonoMomo (USA)
www.kimonomomo.etsy.com

Shibori Dragon (USA)
www.shiboridragon.com

Upcycle Stitches (USA)
www.upcyclestitches.com

A Threaded Needle (Canada)
www.athreadedneedle.com

Sashi.Co (Japan)
en.sashico.com

Yuzawaya (Japan)
www.yuzawaya.co.jp

bibliography

Boro: Threads of Life (Reece/Boudin/Christian), pub. 2014, ISBN 978-2-9536-2793-0

Mottainai: The Fabric of Life (Gallery Kei & Sri), pub. 2011

Boro: Rags and Tatters from the Far North of Japan (Tsuzuki), pub. 2008, ISBN 978-4-7572-1596-2

Nuno no Kioku (Memory of Cloth) (Morita), pub. 2011, ISBN 978-4-8615-2326-7

Kofu ni Mise Rareta Kurashi (Life Attracted to Old Cloth) (publisher: Gakken Interior Mook), pub. 2006, ISBN 4-05-603986-0

Wa no Nuno Tsunagi (Linked Japanese Cloth) (Maeda), pub. 2003, ISBN 978-4-5791-0963-0

Nuno o Tsunagi Hibi (Everyday Patchwork) (Maeda), pub. 2006, ISBN 978-4-5791-1116-9

acknowledgements

I would like to thank the following people for their help in planning and creating this book: all the team at David and Charles publishers; Olympus Thread Mfg. Co. (Japan); my husband Glyn (who stitched the patches on the gadget slipcase, donated his old DIY jeans for the messenger bag, and loaned several pairs of his boro-inspired patched jeans for the Techniques chapter); and the students who have attended my boro workshops over the last decade. The bulk of the work on this book was done during the UK COVID-19 lockdown in spring 2020 and we have had to adapt to a completely distanced method of working. Everyone's patience and skill in working around this has been much appreciated.

about the author

Susan Briscoe began collecting boro by accident in 1991, while working as an assistant English teacher in Yuza-machi, Japan. She has studied many boro pieces in various museums and exhibitions in the UK and Japan, and taught workshops inspired by old boro since 2009. All the old boro items shown in this book are from her personal collection. Susan also specializes in sashiko, kogin, patchwork and quilting, and she is the author of many books on these subjects.

index

A DAVID AND CHARLES BOOK

David and Charles is an imprint of David and Charles, Ltd
Suite A, Tourism House, Pynes Hill, Exeter, EX2 5WT

First published in the UK and USA in 2020

A catalogue record for this book is available from the British Library.

ISBN-13: 9781446308325 paperback
ISBN-13: 9781446379844 EPUB

This book has been printed on paper from approved suppliers and made from pulp from sustainable sources.

Printed in the UK by Pureprint for:
David and Charles, Ltd
Suite A, Tourism House, Pynes Hill, Exeter, EX2 5WT

10 9 8 7 6 5 4 3 2

Publishing Director: Ame Verso
Senior Commissioning Editor: Sarah Callard
Managing Editor: Jessica Cropper
Project Editor: Cheryl Brown
Head of Design: Anna Wade
Book Layout and Design: Sam Staddon
Pre-press Designer: Ali Stark
Art Direction: Laura Woussen
Photography: Jason Jenkins
Illustrations: Kuo Kang Chen
Production Manager: Beverley Richardson

Layout of the digital edition of this book may vary depending on reader hardware and display settings.